W9-APH-925

project management®

MINUTE
10
GUIDE

alpha books
201 West 103rd Street
Indianapolis, IN 46290

A Pearson Education Company

Jeff Davidson

10 Minute Guide to Project Management

International Standard Book Number: 0-02-863966-9
Library of Congress Catalog Card Number: Available upon request.

02 01   8 7 6 5 4 3 2

Interpretation of the printing code: The rightmost number of the first series of numbers is the year of the book's printing; the rightmost number of the second series of numbers is the number of the book's printing. For example, a printing code of 00-1 shows that the first printing occurred in 2000.

Printed in the United States of America

Contents

Introduction

Suppose you are a rising star at work and the boss has given you your first assignment to head up a project. Depending on the nature of the project and what kind of work you do, you might have to engage in a variety of tasks that you haven't tackled before, such as assembling a team to complete the project on time and on budget, mapping out a plan and monitoring your progress at key steps along the way, using appropriate planning tools such as project management software or wall charts, and keeping your team motivated and on target.

Perhaps you have managed projects before, but not recently. Or, you have been given a new kind of project you are not familiar with, and you want to make sure you handle the job right. If so, you've come to the right place. The *10 Minute Guide to Project Management* gives you the essence of what you need to know, in terms of successful project management from A to Z.

True to the series, each lesson can be read and absorbed in about 10 minutes. We cover crucial aspects of project management including plotting out your path, drawing upon age-old and cutting-edge supporting tools, expending your resources carefully, assembling a winning team, monitoring your progress, adjusting course (if you have to), and learning from your experience so that you will be even better at managing other projects in the future.

If you are like many professionals today, you are very busy! Your time is precious. When you're handed a challenging assignment and need some direction, you need it in a hurry. And that is precisely what the *10 Minute Guide to Project Management* offers you, a quick reference tool—divided into 18 crucial aspects of project management—that offers the basics. You will be able to digest a lesson or two each morning if you choose, before everyone else gets to work. Moreover, with this handy pocket guide, you are never more than a few pages away from homing in on the precise information that you need.

So, let's get started on the path to effective project management.

ACKNOWLEDGMENTS

I would like to acknowledge the fine folks at Alpha Books for initiating such a nifty series including the publisher, Marie Butler-Knight, and my editors, Amy Zavatto, Tom Stevens, and Billy Fields.

I would also like to acknowledge Julia Wood for collecting and assembling the brunt of the background and research materials that were fundamental for completing this project, Julia Wood, Matt Mullen, and Jennifer Feinman for expert proofreading, Susan M. Davidson for word processing, and Valerie A. Davidson, now age 10, for consistently being a good girl.

LESSON 1

So You're Going to Manage a Project?

In this lesson, you learn what a project is, essential skills for project managers, and what it takes to be a good project manager.

THE ELEMENTS OF A PROJECT

What exactly is a project? You hear the word used all the time at work, as well as at home. People say, "I am going to add a deck in the backyard. It will be a real project." Or, "Our team's project is to determine consumer preferences in our industry through the year 2010." Or, "I have a little project I would like you to tackle. I think that you can be finished by this afternoon."

TIP

> When you boil it all down, projects can be viewed as having four essential elements: a specific timeframe, an orchestrated approach to co-dependent events, a desired outcome, and unique characteristics.

SPECIFIC TIMEFRAME

Projects are temporary undertakings. In this regard, they are different from ongoing programs that obviously had a beginning, but may not have a desired end, at least for the foreseeable future. Projects can last years or even decades, as in the case of public works programs, feeding the world's hungry, or sending space crafts to other galaxies. But most of the projects that you face in the work-a-day world will be somewhere in the range of hours to weeks, or possibly months, but usually not years or decades. (Moreover, the scope of this book will be limited to projects of short duration, say six months at the most, but usually shorter than that.)

A project begins when some person or group in authority authorizes its beginning. The initiating party has the authority, the budget, and the resources to enable the project to come to fruition, or as Captain Jean Luc Packard of the Starship Enterprise often said, "Make it so." By definition, every project initiated is engaged for a precise period, although those charged with achieving the project's goals often feel as if the project were going on forever. When project goals are completed (the subject of discussion below), a project ends and, invariably, something else takes its place.

TIP

> Much of the effort of the people on a project, and certainly the use of resources, including funds, are directed toward ensuring that the project is designed to achieve the desired outcome and be completed as scheduled in an appropriate manner.

Along the way toward completion or realization of a desired outcome, the project may have interim due dates in which "deliverables" must be completed. Deliverables can take the form of a report, provision of service, a prototype, an actual product, a new procedure, or any one of a number of other forms. Each deliverable and each interim goal achieved helps to ensure that the overall project will be finished on time and on budget.

PLAIN ENGLISH

> **Deliverables**   Something of value generated by a project management team as scheduled, to be offered to an authorizing party, a reviewing committee, client constituent, or other concerned party, often taking the form of a plan, report, prescript procedure, product, or service.

An Orchestrated Approach to Co-dependent Events

Projects involve a series of related events. One event leads to another. Sometimes multiple events are contingent upon other multiple events overlapping in intricate patterns. Indeed, if projects did not involve multiple events, they would not be projects. They would be single tasks or a series of single tasks that are laid out in some sequential pattern.

PLAIN ENGLISH

> **Task** or **event**   A divisible, definable unit of work related to a project, which may or may not include subtasks.

Projects are more involved; some may be so complex that the only way to understand the pattern of interrelated events is to depict them on a chart, or use specially developed project management software. Such tools enable the project manager to see which tasks need to be executed concurrently, versus sequentially, and so on.

PLAIN ENGLISH

Project Manager   An individual who has the responsibility for overseeing all aspects of the day-to-day activities in pursuit of a project goal, including coordinating staff, allocating resources, managing the budget, and coordinating overall efforts to achieve a specific, desired result.

CAUTION

Coordination of events for some projects is so crucial that if one single event is not executed as scheduled, the entire project could be at risk!

Effective project management requires the ability to view the project at hand with a holistic perspective. By seeing the various interrelated project events and activities as part of an overall system, the project manager and project team have a better chance of approaching the project in a coordinated fashion, supporting each other at critical junctures, recognizing where bottle necks and dead ends may occur, and staying focused as a team to ensure effective completion of the project.

PLAIN ENGLISH

Holistic   The organic or functional relations between the part and the whole.

A DESIRED OUTCOME

At the end of each project is the realization of some specific goal or objective. It is not enough to assign a project to someone and say, "See what you can do with this." Nebulous objectives will more than likely lead to a nebulous outcome. A specific objective increases the chances of leading to a specific outcome.

PLAIN ENGLISH

> **Objective**   A desired outcome; something worth striving for; the overarching goal of a project; the reason the project was initiated to begin with.

While there may be one major, clear, desired project objective, in pursuit of it there may be interim project objectives. The objectives of a project management team for a food processing company, for example, might be to improve the quality and taste of the company's macaroni dish. Along the way, the team might conduct taste samples, survey consumers, research competitors, and so on. Completion of each of these events can be regarded as an interim objective toward completion of the overall objective.

In many instances, project teams are charged with achieving a series of increasingly lofty objectives in pursuit of the final, ultimate objective. Indeed, in many cases, teams can only proceed in a stair step fashion to achieve the desired outcome. If they were to proceed in any other manner, they may not be able to develop the skills or insights along the way that will enable them to progress in a productive manner. And just as major league baseball teams start out in spring training by doing calisthenics, warm-up exercises, and reviewing the fundamentals of the game, such as base running, fielding, throwing, bunting and so on, so too are project teams charged with meeting a series of interim objectives and realizing a series of interim outcomes in order to hone their skills and capabilities.

The interim objectives and interim outcomes go by many names. Some people call them goals, some call them milestones, some call them phases, some call them tasks, some call them subtasks. Regardless of the terminology used, the intent is the same: to achieve a desired objective on time and on budget.

PLAIN ENGLISH

Milestone   A significant event or juncture in the project.

Time and money are inherent constraints in the pursuit of any project. If the timeline is not specific—the project can be completed any old time—then it is not a project. It might be a wish, it might be a desire, it might be an aim, it might be a long held notion, but it is not a project. By assigning a specific timeframe to a project, project team members can mentally acclimate themselves to the rigors inherent in operating under said constrictions.

PLAIN ENGLISH

Timeline   The scheduled start and stop times for a subtask, task, phase, or entire project.

CAUTION

Projects are often completed beyond the timeframe initially allotted. Nevertheless, setting the timeframe is important. If it had not been set, the odds of the project being completed anywhere near the originally earmarked period would be far less.

Although the budget for a project is usually imposed upon a project manager by someone in authority, or by the project manager himself—as with the timeframe constraint—a budget serves as a highly useful and necessary constraint of another nature. It would be nice to have deep pockets for every project that you engage in, but the reality for most organizations and most people is that budgetary limits must be set. And it is just as well.

TIP

> Budgetary limits help ensure efficiency. If you know that you only have so many dollars to spend, you spend those dollars more judiciously than you would if you had double or triple that amount.

The great architect Frank Lloyd Wright once said, "Man built most nobly when limitations were at their greatest." Since each architectural achievement is nothing more than a complex project, Wright's observation is as applicable for day-to-day projects routinely faced by managers as it is for a complex, multinational undertaking.

UNIQUE CHARACTERISTICS

If you have been assigned a multipart project, the likes of which you have never undertaken before, independent of your background and experience, that project is an original, unique undertaking for you. Yet, even if you have just completed something of a similar nature the month before, the new assignment would still represent an original project, with its own set of challenges. Why? Because as time passes, society changes, technology changes, and your workplace changes.

Suppose you are asked to manage the orientation project for your company's new class of recruits. There are ten of them, and they will be with you for a three-week period, just like the group before them. The company's orientation materials have been developed for a long time, they are excellent, and, by and large, they work.

You have excellent facilities and budget, and though limited, they have proven to be adequate, and you are up for the task. Nevertheless, this project is going to be unique, because you haven't encountered these ten people before. Their backgrounds and experiences, the way that they interact with one another and with you, and a host of other factors ensure that challenges will arise during this three-week project, some of which will represent unprecedented challenges.

PLAIN ENGLISH

> **Project**   The allocation of resources over a specific timeframe and the coordination of interrelated events to accomplish an overall objective while meeting both predictable and unique challenges.

PROJECT PLANNING

All effectively managed projects involve the preparation of the project plan. This is the fundamental document that spells out what is to be achieved, how it is to be achieved, and what resources will be necessary. In *Projects and Trends in the 1990s and the 21st Century*, author Jolyon Hallows says, "The basic project document is the project plan. The project lives and breathes and changes as the project progresses or fails." The basic components of the project, according to Hallows, are laid out in the figure below.

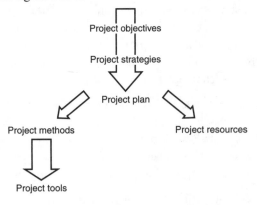

© Jolyon Hallows

Basic project components.

"With the plan as a road map, telling us how to get from one point to another," says Hallows, "a good project manager recognizes from the outset that a project plan is far more than an academic exercise or tool for appeasing upper management. It is the blueprint for the entire scope of the project, a vital document which is referred to frequently, often updated on-the-fly, and something without which the project manager cannot proceed."

PLAIN ENGLISH

Scope of the project or **scope of work**   The level of activity and effort necessary to complete a project and achieve the desired outcome as measured by staff hours, staff days, resources consumed, and funds spent.

Prior to laying out the project plan (the subject of Lesson 4, "Laying Out Your Plan"), the manager starts with a rough pre-plan—this could take the form of an outline, a proposal, a feasibility study, or simply a memorandum. The preplan triggers the project.

From there, a more detailed project plan is drawn up that includes the delegation of tasks among project team members, the identification of interim objectives, which may also be called goals, milestones, or tasks, all laid out in sequence for all concerned with the project to see.

Once the plan commences and the project team members, as well as the project manager, begin to realize what they are really up against, the project plan is invariably modified. Hallows says that "all plans are guesses to some extent. Good plans are good guesses, bad plans are bad guesses." No plans are analogous to horrible guesses.

TIP

Any plan is better than no plan, since no plan doesn't lead anywhere.

IMPLEMENTATION

Following the preparation of a formal project plan, project execution or implementation ensues. This is where the excitement begins. If drawing up the project plan was a somewhat dry process, implementing it is anything but. Here, for the first time, you put your plan into action. You consult the plan as if it were your trail map, assigning this task to person A, this task to person B, and so on. What was once only on paper or on disc now corresponds to action in the real world. People are doing things as a result of your plan.

If your team is charged with developing a new software product, some members begin by examining the code of previous programs, while others engage in market research, while still others contemplate the nature of computing two years out.

If your team is charged with putting up a new building, some begin by surveying the area, others by marking out the ground, some by mixing cement and laying foundation, others by erecting scaffolding, while yet others may be redirecting traffic.

If your project involves successfully training your company's sales division on how to use a new type of hand held computer, initial implementation activities may involve scheduling the training sessions, developing the lesson plans, finding corollaries between the old procedures and the new, testing the equipment, and so on.

TIP

> Regardless of what type of project is at hand, the implementation phase is a period of high energy and excitement as team members begin to realize that the change is actually going to happen and that what they are doing will make a difference.

CONTROL

From implementation on, the project manager's primary task becomes that of monitoring progress. Because this is covered extensively in Lessons 6, 7, 9, and 11, suffice it to say here that the effective project manager continually examines what has been accomplished to date; how that jibes with the project plan; what modifications, if any, need to be made to the project plan; and what needs to be done next. He or she also needs to consider what obstacles and roadblocks may be further along the path, the morale and motivation of his or her staff, and how much of the budget has been expended, versus how much remains.

CAUTION

> Monitoring progress often becomes the full time obsession of the project manager intent on bringing the project in on time and on budget. In doing so, however, some managers lose the personal touch with team members.

Steadfastness in monitoring the project is but one of the many traits necessary to be successful in project management, and that is the subject of our exploration in Lesson 2, "What Makes a Good Project Manager?"

POSSIBLE PROJECT PLAYERS

The following are the types of participants you may encounter in the course of a project:

Authorizing Party   Initiates the project. (Often called a sponsor, an unfortunate term, since after initiation, many "sponsors" offer very little sponsorship).

Stakeholder   Typically someone like a senior manager, business developer, client or other involved party. There may be many stakeholders on a project.

Work Manager   Responsible for planning activities within projects and servicing requests.

Administrative Manager   Tends to the staff by assuring that standard activities, such as training, vacation and other planned activities are in the schedules.

Project Manager   Initiates, then scopes and plans work and resources.

Team Member   A staff member who performs the work to be managed.

Software Guru   Helps install, run, and apply software.

Project Director   Supervises one or more project managers.

THE 30-SECOND RECAP

- A project is a unique undertaking to achieve a specific objective and desired outcome by coordinating events and activities within a specific time frame.

- The project plan is the fundamental document directing all activities in pursuit of the desired objective. The plan may change as time passes, but nevertheless, it represents the project manager's continuing view on what needs to be done by whom and when.

- Planning leads to implementation, and implementation requires control. The effective project manager constantly monitors progress for the duration of the project. For many, it becomes a near obsession.

LESSON 2
What Makes a Good Project Manager?

In this lesson, you will learn the traits of successful project managers, the reasons that project managers succeed, and the reasons that they fail.

A Doer, not a Bystander

If you are assigned the task of project manager within your organization, consider this: You were probably selected because you exhibited the potential to be an effective project manager. (Or conversely, there was no one else around, so you inherited the task!) In essence, a project manager is an active doer, not a passive bystander. As you learned in Lesson 1, "So You're Going to Manage a Project?" a big portion of the project manager's responsibility is planning—mapping out how a project will be undertaken; anticipating obstacles and roadblocks; making course adjustments; and continually determining how to allocate human, technological, or monetary resources.

If you have a staff, from one person to ten or more, then in addition to daily supervision of the work being performed, you are probably going to be involved in some type of training. The training might be once, periodic, or nonstop. As the project progresses, you find yourself having to be a motivator, a cheerleader, possibly a disciplinarian, an empathetic listener, and a sounding board. As you guessed, not everyone is qualified to (or wants to) serve in such capacity. On top of these responsibilities, you may be the key contact point for a variety of vendors, suppliers, subcontractors, and supplemental teams within your own organization.

CAUTION

Whether you work for a multibillion dollar organization or a small business, chances are you don't have all the administrative support you would like to have. In addition to these tasks, too many project managers today also must engage in a variety of administrative duties, such as making copies, print outs, or phone calls on mundane matters.

If your staff lets you down or is cut back at any time during the project (and this is almost inevitable), you end up doing some of the tasks that you had assigned to others on top of planning, implementing, and controlling the project.

PLAIN ENGLISH

Subcontract An agreement with an outside vendor for specific services, often to alleviate a project management team of a specific task, tasks, or an entire project.

Many Hats All the Time

The common denominator among all successful project managers everywhere is the ability to develop a "whatever it takes" attitude. Suppose

- Several of your project team members get pulled off the project to work for someone else in your organization. You will make do.

- You learn that an essential piece of equipment that was promised to you is two weeks late. You will improvise.

- You discover that several key assumptions you made during the project planning and early implementation phases turned out to be wildly off the mark. You will adjust.

- One-third of the way into the project a mini-crisis develops in your domestic life. You will get by.

CAUTION

Chances are that you're going to be wearing many hats, several of which you can not anticipate at the start of a project.

Although the role and responsibility of a project manager may vary somewhat from project to project and from organization to organization, you may be called upon to perform one of these recurring duties and responsibilities:

- Draw up the project plan, possibly present and "sell" the project to those in authority.

- Interact with top management, line managers, project team members, supporting staff, and administrative staff.

- Procure project resources, allocate them to project staff, coordinate their use, ensure that they are being maintained in good working order, and surrender them upon project completion.

- Interact with outside vendors, clients, and other project managers and project staff within your organization.

- Initiate project implementation, continually monitor progress, review interim objectives or milestones, make course adjustments, view and review budgets, and continually monitor all project resources.

- Supervise project team members, manage the project team, delegate tasks, review execution of tasks, provide feedback, and delegate new tasks.

- Identify opportunities, identify problems, devise appropriate adjustments, and stay focused on the desired outcome.

- Handle interteam strife, minimize conflicts, resolve differences, instill a team atmosphere, and continually motivate team members to achieve superior performance.

- Prepare interim presentations for top management, offer a convincing presentation, receive input and incorporate it, review results with project staff, and make still more course adjustments.

- Make the tough calls, such as having to remove project team members, ask project team members to work longer hours on short notice, reassign roles and responsibilities to the disappointment of some, discipline team members as may be necessary, and resolve personality-related issues affecting the team.

- Consult with advisors, mentors, and coaches, examine the results of previous projects, draw upon previously unidentified or underused resources, and remain as balanced and objective as possible.

PRINCIPLES TO STEER YOU

In his book, *Managing Projects in Organizations*, J. D. Frame identifies five basic principles that, if followed, will "help project professionals immeasurably in their efforts."

BE CONSCIOUS OF WHAT YOU ARE DOING

Don't be an accidental project manager. Seat-of-the-pants efforts may work when you are undertaking a short-term task, particularly something you are doing alone. However, for longer-term tasks that involve working with others and with a budget, being an accidental manager will get you into trouble.

Remember that a project, by definition, is something that has a unique aspect to it. Even if you are building your 15th chicken coop in a row, the grading of the land or composition of the soil might be different from that of the first 14. As Frame points out, many projects are hard enough to manage even when you know what you are doing. They are nearly impossible to manage by happenstance. Thus, it behooves you to draw up an effective project plan and use it as an active, vital document.

INVEST HEAVILY IN THE FRONT-END SPADE WORK

Get it right the first time. How many times do you buy a new technology item, bring it to your office or bring it home, and start pushing the buttons without reading the instructions? If you are honest, the answer is all too often.

CAUTION

> Jumping in too quickly in project management is going to get you into big trouble in a hurry.

Particularly if you are the type of person who likes to leap before you look, as project manager you need to understand and recognize the value of slowing down, getting your facts in order, and then proceeding. Frame says, "By definition, projects are unique, goal-oriented systems; consequently they are complex. Because they are complex, they cannot be managed effectively in an offhand and ad-hoc fashion. They must be carefully selected and carefully planned." Most importantly, he says, "A good deal of thought must be directed at determining how they should be structured. Care taken at the outset of a project to do things right will generally pay for itself handsomely."

CAUTION

> For many project managers, particularly first-time project managers, investing in front-end spadework represents a personal dilemma—the more time spent up front, the less likely they are to feel that they're actually managing the project.

Too many professionals today, reeling from the effects of our information overloaded society, feeling frazzled by all that competes for their time and attention, want to dive right into projects much the same way they dive into many of their daily activities and short-term tasks. What works well for daily activity or short-term tasks can prove disastrous when others are counting on you, there is a budget involved, top management is watching, and any falls you make along the way will be quite visible.

Anticipate the Problems That Will Inevitably Arise

The tighter your budget and time frames, or the more intricate the involvement of the project team, the greater the probability that problems will ensue. While the uniqueness of your project may foreshadow the emergence of unforeseen problems, inevitably many of the problems that you will experience are somewhat predictable. These include, but are not limited to:

- Missing interim milestones

- Having resources withdrawn midstream

- Having one or more project team members who are not up to the tasks assigned

- Having the project objective(s) altered midstream

- Falling behind schedule

- Finding yourself over budget

- Learning about a hidden project agenda halfway into the project

- Losing steam, motivation, or momentum

Frame says that by reviewing these inevitable realities and anticipating their emergence, you are in a far better position to deal with them once they occur. Moreover, as you become increasingly adept as a project manager, you might even learn to use such situations to your advantage. (More on this in Lesson 14, "Learning from Your Experience.")

Go Beneath Surface Illusions

Dig deeply to find the facts in situations. Frame says, "Project managers are continually getting into trouble because they accept things at face value. If your project involves something that requires direct interaction with your company's clients, and you erroneously believe that you know exactly what the clients want, you may be headed for major problems."

CAUTION

> All too often, the client says one thing but really means another and offers you a rude awakening by saying, "We didn't ask for this, and we can't use it."

One effective technique used by project managers to find the real situation in regard to others upon whom the project outcome depends is as follows:

- Identify all participants involved in the project, even those with tangential involvement.

- List the possible goals that each set of participants could have in relation to the completion of the project.

- Now, list all possible subagendas, hidden goals, and unstated aspirations.

- Determine the strengths and weaknesses of your project plan and your project team in relation to the goals and hidden agendas of all other parties to the project.

In this manner, you are less likely both to encounter surprises and to find yourself scrambling to recover from unexpected jolts.

My friend Peter Hicks, who is a real-estate developer from Massachusetts, says that when he engages in a project with another party, one of the most crucial exercises he undertakes is a complete mental walk-through of everything that the party

- Wants to achieve as a result of this project

- Regards as an extreme benefit

- May have as a hidden agenda

- Can do to let him down

The last item is particularly telling. Peter finds that by sketching out all the ways that the other party may not fulfill his obligations, he is in a far better position to proceed, should any of them come true. In essence, he takes one hundred percent of the responsibility for ensuring that the project outcomes that he desired will be achieved. To be sure, this represents more work, perhaps 50 percent or more of what most project managers are willing to undertake.

You have to ask yourself the crucial question: If you are in project management, and you aim to succeed, are you willing to adopt the whatever-it-takes mindset? By this, I don't mean that you engage in illegal, immoral, or socially reprehensible behavior. Rather, it means a complete willingness to embrace the reality of the situation confronting you, going as deeply below the surface as you can to ferret out the true dynamics of the situation before you, and marshaling the resources necessary to be successful.

BE AS FLEXIBLE AS POSSIBLE

Don't get sucked into unnecessary rigidity and formality. This principle of effective project management can be seen as one that is counterbalanced to the four discussed thus far. Once a project begins, an effective project manager wants to maintain a firm hand while having the ability to roll with the punches. You have heard the old axiom about the willow tree being able to withstand hurricane gusts exceeding 100 miles per hour, while the branches of the more rigid spruce and oak trees surrounding it snap in half.

TIP

> The ability to "bend, but not break" has been the hallmark of the effective manager and project manager in all of business and industry, government and institution, education, health care, and service industries.

In establishing a highly detailed project plan that creates a situation where practically nothing is left to fortune, one can end up creating a nightmarish, highly constrictive bureaucracy. We have seen this happen all too frequently at various levels of government. Agencies empowered to serve its citizenry end up being only marginally effective, in servitude to the web of bureaucratic entanglement and red tape that has grown, obscuring the view of those entrusted to serve.

Increasingly, in our high tech age of instantaneous information and communication, where intangible project elements outnumber the tangible by a hearty margin, the wise project manager knows the value of staying flexible, constantly gathering valuable feedback, and responding accordingly.

SEVEN WAYS TO SUCCEED AS A PROJECT MANAGER

Now that you have a firm understanding of the kinds of issues that befall a project manager, let's take a look at seven ways in particular that project managers can succeed, followed by seven ways that project managers can fail.

- **Learn to use project management tools effectively**   As you will see in Lessons 10, "Choosing Project Management Software," and 11, "A Sampling of Popular Programs," such a variety of wondrous project managing software tools exist today that it is foolhardy to proceed in a project of any type of complexity without having a rudimentary understanding of available software tools, if not an intermediate to advanced understanding of them. Project management tools today can be of such enormous aid that they can mean the difference between a project succeeding or failing.

- **Be able to give and receive criticism**   Giving criticism effectively is not easy. There is a fine line between upsetting a team member's day and offering constructive feedback that will help the team member and help the project. Likewise, the ability to receive criticism is crucial for project managers.

TIP

As the old saying goes, it is easy to avoid criticism: Say nothing, do nothing, and be nothing. If you are going to move mountains, you are going to have to accept a little flack.

- **Be receptive to new procedures**   You don't know everything, and thank goodness. Team members, other project managers, and those who authorize the project to begin with can provide valuable input, including new directions and new procedures. Be open to them, because you just might find a way to slash $20,000 and three months off of your project cost.

- **Manage your time well**   Speaking of time, if you personally are not organized, dawdle on low-level issues, and find yourself perpetually racing the clock, how are you going to manage your project, a project team, and achieve the desired outcome on time and on budget? My earlier book in this series, *The 10-Minute Guide to Time Management* will help you enormously in this area.

- **Be effective at conducting meetings**   Meetings are a necessary evil in the event of completing projects, with the exception of solo projects. A good short text on this topic is *Breakthrough Business Meetings* by Robert Levasseur. This book covers the fundamentals of meetings in a succinct, enjoyable manner, and can make any project manager an effective meeting manager in relatively short order.

- **Hone your decision-making skills**   As a project manager you won't have the luxury of sitting on the fence for very long in relation to issues crucial to the success of your project. Moreover, your staff looks to you for yes, no, left, and right decisions. If you waffle here and there, you are giving the signal that you are not really in control. As with other things in project management, decision-making is a skill that can be learned. However, the chances are high that you already have the decision-making capability that you need. It is why you were chosen to manage this project to begin with. It is also why you have been able to achieve what you have in your career up to this point.

TIP

> Trusting yourself is a vital component to effective project management.

- **Maintain a sense of humor**   Stuff is going to go wrong, things are going to happen out of the blue, the weird and the wonderful are going to pass your way. You have to maintain a sense of humor so that you don't do damage to your health, to your team, to your organization, and to the project itself. Sometimes, not always, the best response to a breakdown is to simply let out a good laugh. Take a walk, stretch, renew yourself, and then come back and figure out what you are going to do next. Colin Powell, in his book *My American Journey*, remarked that in almost all circumstances, "things will look better in the morning."

SEVEN WAYS TO FAIL AS A PROJECT MANAGER

Actually, there are hundreds and hundreds of ways to fail as a project manager. The following seven represent those that I have seen too often in the work place:

- **Fail to address issues immediately**   Two members of your project team can't stand each other and cooperation is vital to the success of the project. As project manager, you must address the issue head on. Either find a way that they can work together professionally, if not amicably, or modify roles and assignments. Whatever you do, don't let the issue linger. It will only come back to haunt you further along.

- **Reschedule too often**   As the project develops, you can certainly change due dates, assignments, and schedules. Recognize though, that there is a cost every time you make a change, and if you ask your troops to keep up with too many changes you are inviting mistakes, missed deadlines, confusion, and possibly hidden resentment.

- **Be content with reaching milestones on time, but ignore quality**   Too often, project managers in the heat of battle, focused on completing the project on time and within budget, don't focus sufficiently on the quality of work done.

CAUTION

A series of milestones that you reach with less than desired quality work adds up to a project that misses the mark.

- **Too much focus on project administration and not enough on project management**   In this high tech era with all manner of sophisticated project management software, it is too easy to fall in love with project administration—making sure that equipment arrives, money is allocated, and assignments are doled out to the neglect of project management, taking in the big picture of what the team is up against, where they are heading, and what they are trying to accomplish.

- **Micromanage rather than manage**   This is reflected in the project manager who plays his cards close to his chest, and retains most of the tasks himself, or at least the ones he deems to be crucial, rather than delegating. The fact that you have staff implies that there are many tasks and responsibilities that you should not be handling. On the other hand, if you should decide to handle it all, be prepared to stay every night until 10:30, give up your weekends, and generally be in need of a life.

CAUTION

> Micromanaging isn't pretty. The most able managers know when to share responsibilities with others and to keep focused on the big picture.

- **Adapt new tools too readily**   If you are managing a project for the first time and counting on a tool that you have not used before, you are incurring a double risk. Here's how it works. Managing a project for the first time is a single risk. Using a project tool for the first time is a single risk. Both levels of risk are acceptable. You can be a first-time project manager using tools that you are familiar with, or you can be a veteran project manager using tools for the first time. However, it is unacceptable to be a first-time project manager using project tools for the first time.

PLAIN ENGLISH

> **Risk**   The degree to which a project or portions of a project are in jeopardy of not being completed on time and on budget, and, most importantly, the probability that the desired outcome will not be achieved.

- **Monitor project progress intermittently**   Just as a ship that is off course one degree at the start of a voyage ends up missing the destination by a thousand miles, so too a slight deviation in course in the early rounds of your project can result in having to do double or triple time to get back on track. Hence, monitoring progress is a project-long responsibility. It is important at the outset for the reasons just mentioned, and it is important in mid and late stages to avoid last-minute surprises.

The 30-Second Recap

- Project managers are responsible for planning, supervising, administering, motivating, training, coordinating, listening, readjusting, and achieving.

- Five basic principles of effective project management include being conscious of what you are doing, investing heavily in the front-end work, anticipating problems, going beneath the surface, and staying flexible.

- Project managers who succeed are able to effectively give and receive criticism, know how to conduct a meeting, maintain a sense of humor, manage their time well, are open to new procedures, and use project management support tools effectively.

- Project managers who fail let important issues fester, fail to focus on quality, get too involved with administration and neglect management, micromanage rather than delegate, rearrange tasks or schedules too often, and rely too heavily on unfamiliar tools.

LESSON 3

What Do You Want to Accomplish?

In this lesson, you learn how important it is to fully understand the project, what kinds of projects lend themselves to project management, and why it is important to start with the end in mind.

TO LEAD AND TO HANDLE CRISES

Project managers come in many varieties, but if you were to boil down the two primary characteristics of project managers they would be

- A project manager's ability to lead a team. This is largely dependent upon the managerial and personal characteristics of the project manager.

- A project manager's ability to handle the critical project issues. This involves the project manager's background, skills, and experience in handling these and similar issues.

If you could only pick one set of attributes for a project manager, either being good at the people side of managing projects or being good at the technical side of managing projects, which do you suppose, over the broad span of all projects ever undertaken, has proven to be the most valuable? You guessed it, the people side.

In his book, *Information Systems Project Management*, author Jolyon Hallows observes, "Hard though it may be to admit, the people side of projects is more important than the technical side. Those who are anointed or appointed as project managers because of their technical capability have to overcome the temptation of focusing on technical issues rather than the people or political issue that invariably becomes paramount to project success."

TIP

> If you are managing the project alone, you can remain as technically oriented as you like.

Even on a solo project, given that you will end up having to report to others, the people side never entirely goes away. Your ability to relate to the authorizing party, fellow project managers, and any staff people who may only tangentially be supporting your efforts can spell the difference between success and failure for your project.

KEY QUESTIONS

On the road to determining what you want to accomplish, it is important to understand your project on several dimensions. Hallows suggests asking key questions, including:

- Do I understand the project's justification? Why does someone consider this project to be important? If you are in a large organization, this means contemplating why the authorizing party initiated the assignment and whom he or she had to sell before you were brought into the picture.

- Do I understand the project's background? It is unlikely that the project exists in a vacuum. Probe to find out what has been done in this area previously, if anything. If the project represents a new method or procedure, what is it replacing? Is the project a high priority item within your organization, or is it something that is not necessarily crucial to continuing operations?

- Do I understand the project's politics? Who stands to benefit from the success of the full completion of this project?

Whose feathers may be ruffled by achieving the desired out-come? Who will be supportive? Who will be resistant?

- Do I understand who the players are and the role they will take? Who can and will contribute their effort and expertise to the project? Who will be merely bystanders, and who will be indifferent?

PLAIN ENGLISH

Politics   The relationship of two or more people with one another, including the degree of power and influence that the parties have over one another.

Hallows says that projects involve "the dynamic mix of people with different interests, philosophies, values, approaches and priorities. One of your main functions as a project manger," particularly in regards to what you want to accomplish, is to "ensure that this mix becomes coherent and drives the project forward." He warns that, "the alternative is chaos."

CAUTION

Project management is not for the meek. At times, you will have to be tough and kick some proverbial derriere. As a project manager, you become the human representative for the project. Think of the project as taking on a life of its own, with you as its spokesperson.

OKAY, SO WHAT ARE WE ATTEMPTING TO DO?

A post mortem of projects that failed reveals that all too often the pro-jects were begun "on the run," rather than taking a measured approach to determining exactly what needs to be accomplished. Too many projects start virtually in motion, before a precise definition of what needs to be achieved is even concocted.

In some organizations, projects are routinely rushed from the beginning. Project managers and teams are given near-impossible deadlines, and the only alternative is for the project players to throw their time and energy at the project, working late into the evening and on weekends. All of this is in the vainglorious attempt to produce results in record time and have "something" to show to top management, a client, the VP of product development, the sales staff, or whomever.

In properly defining the project, Hallows suggests a few basic questions, including the following:

- **Have I defined the project deliverables?** The deliverables (as discussed in Lesson 1, "So You're Going to Manage a Project?") could also be analogous to outcomes, are often associated with project milestones, and represent the evidence or proof that the project team is meeting the challenge or resolving the issue for which they were initially assembled.

TIP

Teams that start in a rush, and accelerate the pace from there, run the risk of being more focused on producing *a* deliverable instead of *the* deliverable. The solution is to define precisely what needs to be done and then to stick to the course of action that will lead to the accomplishment of the goal.

- **Have I established the scope—both system and project?** This involves determining exactly the level of effort required for all aspects of the project, and often plotting the scope and required effort out on a wall chart or using project management software (the topic of Lessons 7, 8, 10, and 11).

- **Have I determined how deliverables will be reviewed and approved?** It is one thing to produce a deliverable on time, is quite another to have the air kicked out of your tires because the reviewing body used criteria that were foreign to you. The remedy is to ensure at the outset that everyone is on the same page in terms of what is to be accomplished. In that regard, it pays to spend more time at the outset than some project managers are willing to spend to determine the deliverables' review and approval processes to which the project manager and project team will be subject.

TIP

> Abraham Lincoln once said that if he had eight hours to cut down a tree he would spend six hours sharpening the saw.

TASKS VERSUS OUTCOMES

One of the recurring problems surrounding the issue of "What is it that needs to be accomplished?" is over-focusing on the project's tasks, as opposed to the project's desired outcome. Project managers who jump into a project too quickly sometimes become enamored by bells and whistles associated with project tasks, rather than critically identifying the specific, desired results that the overall project should achieve. The antidote to this trap is to start with the end in mind, an age-old method for ensuring that all project activities are related to the desired outcome.

TIP

> By having a clear vision of the desired end, all decisions made by the project staff at all points along the trail will have a higher probability of being in alignment with the desired end.

The desired end is never nebulous. It can be accurately described. It is targeted to be achieved within a specific timeframe at a specific cost. The end is quantifiable. It meets the challenge or solves the problem for which the project management team was originally assembled. As I pointed out in my book, *The Complete Idiot's Guide to Reaching Your Goals*, it pays to start from the ending date of a project and work back to the present, indicating the tasks and subtasks you need to undertake and when you need to undertake them.

PLAIN ENGLISH

Subtask   A slice of a complete task; a divisible unit of a larger task. Usually, a series of subtasks leads to the completion of a task.

TIP

Starting from the ending date of a project is a highly useful procedure because when you proceed in reverse, you establish realistic interim goals that can serve as project targets dates.

TELLING QUESTIONS

My co-author for two previous books, including *Marketing Your Consulting and Professional Services* (John Wiley & Sons) and *Getting New Clients* (John Wiley & Sons), is Richard A. Connor. In working on projects with professional service firms, Richard used to ask, "How will you and I know when I have done the job to your satisfaction?"

Some clients were disarmed by this question; they had never been asked it before. Inevitably, answers began to emerge. Clients would say things such as:

- Our accounting and record-keeping costs will decline by 10 percent from those of last year.

- We will retain for at least two years a higher percentage of our new recruits than occurred with our previous recruiting class.

- We will receive five new client inquiries per week, starting immediately.

- Fifteen percent of the proposals we write will result in signed contracts, as opposed to our traditional norm of 11 percent.

Richard Connor's question can be adopted by all project managers as well.

"How will my project team and I know that we have completed the project to the satisfaction of those charged with assessing our efforts?" The response may turn out to be multipart, but invariably the answer homes in on the essential question for all project managers who choose to be successful: "What needs to be accomplished?"

DESIRED OUTCOMES THAT LEND THEMSELVES TO PROJECT MANAGEMENT

Almost any quest in the business world can be handled by applying project management principles. If you work for a large manufacturing, sales, or engineering concern, especially in this ultra-competitive age, there are an endless number of worthwhile projects, among them:

- To reduce inventory holding costs by 25 percent by creating more effective, just-in-time inventory delivery systems

- To comply fully with environmental regulations, while holding operating costs to no more than one percent of the company's three-year norm

- To reduce the "time to market" for new products from an average of 182 days to 85 days

- To increase the average longevity of employees from 2.5 years to 2.75 years

- To open an office in Atlanta and to have it fully staffed by the 15th of next month

If you are in a personal service firm, one of the many projects that you might entertain might include the following:

- To get five new appointments per month with qualified prospects

- To initiate a complete proposal process system by June 30

- To design, test, and implement the XYZ research project in this quarter

- To develop preliminary need scenarios in our five basic target industries

- To assemble our initial contact mailing package and begin the first test mailing within ten days

If you are an entrepreneur or work in an entrepreneurial firm, the types of projects you might tackle include the following:

- To find three joint-venture partners within the next quarter

- To replace the phone system within one month without any service disruption

- To reduce delivery expense by at least 18 percent by creating more circuitous delivery routes

- To create a database/dossier of our 10 most active clients

- To develop a coordinated 12-month advertising plan

Finally, if you are working alone, or simply seeking to rise in your career, the kinds of projects you may want to tackle include the following:

- To earn $52,000 in the next 12 months

- To be transferred to the Hong Kong division of the company by next April

- To have a regular column in the company newsletter (or online 'zine) by next quarter

- To be mentioned in *Wired* magazine this year

- To publish your first book within six months

THE 30-SECOND RECAP

- Too many project managers have an inclination to leap into the project at top speed, without precisely defining what it is that needs to be accomplished and how project deliverables will be assessed by others who are crucial to the project's success.

- Project managers who are people oriented fare better than project managers who are task oriented, because people represent the most critical element in the accomplishment of most projects. A people-oriented project manager can learn elements of task management, whereas task-oriented managers are seldom effective at becoming people-oriented managers.

- It pays to start with the end in mind, to get a clear focus of what is to be achieved, and to better guide all decisions and activities undertaken by members of the project team.

- To know if you're on track, ask the telling question, "How will you and I know when I have done the job to your satisfaction?"

LESSON 4

Laying Out Your Plan

In this lesson, you learn the prime directive of project managers, all about plotting your course, initiating a work breakdown structure, and the difference between action and results (results mean deliverables).

NO SURPRISES

For other than self-initiated projects, it is tempting to believe that the most important aspect of a project is to achieve the desired outcome on time and on budget. As important as that is, there is something even more important. As you initiate, engage in, and proceed with your project, you want to be sure that you do not surprise the authorizing party or any other individuals who have a stake in the outcome of your project.

TIP

Keeping others informed along the way, as necessary, is your prime directive.

When you keep stakeholders "in the information loop," you accomplish many important things. For one, you keep anxiety levels to a minimum. If others get regular reports all along as to how your project is proceeding, then they don't have to make inquiries. They don't have to be constantly checking up. They don't have to be overly concerned.

PLAIN ENGLISH

> **Stakeholder** Those who have a vested interest in having a project succeed. Stakeholders may include the authorizing party, top management, other department and division heads within an organization, other project managers and project management teams, clients, constituents, and parties external to an organization.

Alternatively, by reporting to others on a regular basis, you keep yourself and the project in check. After all, if you are making progress according to plan, then keeping the others informed is a relatively cheerful process. And, having to keep them informed is a safeguard against your allowing the project to meander.

What do the stakeholders want to know? They want to know the project status, whether you are on schedule, costs to date, and the overall project outlook in regards to achieving the desired outcome. They also want to know the likelihood of project costs exceeding the budget, the likelihood that the schedule may get off course, any anticipated problems, and most importantly, any impediments that may loom, or that may threaten the ability of the project team to achieve the desired outcome.

TIP

> The more you keep others in the loop, the higher your credibility will be as a project manager.

You don't need to issue reports constantly, such as on the hour, or even daily in some cases. Depending on the nature of the project, the length, the interests of the various stakeholders, and your desired outcome, reporting daily, every few days, weekly or biweekly may be appropriate. For projects of three months or more, weekly is probably sufficient. For a project of only a couple of weeks, daily status reports might be appropriate. For a long-term project running a half a year or more, biweekly or semimonthly reports might be appropriate. The prevailing notion is that the wise project manager never allows stakeholders to be surprised.

THE HOLY GRAIL AND THE GOLDEN FLEECE

Carefully scoping out the project and laying out an effective project plan minimizes the potential for surprises. A good plan is the Holy Grail that leads you to the Golden Fleece (or the gold at the end of the rainbow, or whatever metaphor you would like to substitute). It indicates everything that you can determine up to the present that needs to be done on the project to accomplish the desired outcome. It provides clarity and direction. It helps you to determine if you are where you need to be, and if not, what it will take to get there.

Any plan (good or bad) is better than no plan. At least with a bad plan you have the potential to upgrade and improve it. With no plan, you are like a boat adrift at sea, with no compass, no sexton, and clouds covering the whole night sky so you can't even navigate by the stars.

FROM NOTHING TO SOMETHING

Perhaps you were lucky. Perhaps the authorizing party gave you an outline, or notes, or a chart of some sort to represent the starting point for you to lay out your plan. Perhaps some kind of feasibility study, corporate memo, or quarterly report served as the forerunner to your project plan, spelling out needs and opportunities of the organization that now represent clues to as to what you need to do on your project.

All too often, no such preliminary documents are available. You get your marching orders from an eight-minute conference with your boss, via email, or over the phone. When you press your boss for some documentation, he or she pulls out a couple of pages from a file folder.

Whatever the origin of your project, you have to start somewhere. As you learned in the last lesson, the mindset of the effective project manager is to start with the end in mind.

- What is the desired final outcome?

- When does it need to be achieved?

- How much can you spend toward its accomplishments?

By starting with major known elements of the project, you begin to fill in your plan, in reverse (as discussed in Lesson 3, "What Do You Want to Accomplish?"), leading back to this very day. We'll cover the use of software in Lessons 10, "Choosing Project Management Software," and 11, "A Sampling of Popular Programs." For now, let's proceed as if pen and paper were all you had. Later, you can transfer the process to a computer screen.

A Journey of a 1000 Miles ...

In laying out your plan, it may become apparent that you have 10 steps, 50 steps, or 150 or more. Some people call each step a task, although I like to use the term event, because not each step represents a pure task. Sometimes each step merely represents something that has to happen. Subordinate activities to the events or tasks are subtasks. There can be numerous subtasks to each task or event, and if you really want to get fancy, there can be sub-subtasks.

TIP

> In laying out your plan, your major challenge as project manager is to ascertain the relationship of different tasks or events to one another and to coordinate them so that the project is executed in a cost-effective and efficient manner.

The primary planning tools in plotting your path are the work breakdown structure (WBS), the Gantt chart, and the PERT/CPM chart (also known as the critical path method), which represents a schedule network. This lesson focuses on the work breakdown structure. We'll get to the other structures in subsequent Lessons 7, "Gantt Charts," and 8, "PERT/CPM Charts."

PLAIN ENGLISH

Work breakdown structure   A complete depiction of all of the tasks necessary to achieve successful project completion. Project plans that delineate all the tasks that must be accomplished to successfully complete a project from which scheduling, delegating, and budgeting are derived.

PLAIN ENGLISH

Path   A chronological sequence of tasks, each dependent on predecessors.

YOU AND ME AGAINST THE WORLD?

So, here you are. Maybe you are all alone and staring at a blank page, or maybe your boss is helping you. Maybe an assistant project manager or someone who will be on the project management team is helping you lay out your plan.

CAUTION

Not getting regular feedback is risky. If there is someone working with you, or if you have someone who can give you regular feedback, it is to your extreme benefit.

Depending on the duration and complexity of your project, it is darned difficult to lay out a comprehensive plan that takes into account all aspects of the project, all critical events, associated subtasks, and the coordination of all. Said another way, if you can get any help in plotting your path, do it!

In laying out your plan, look at the big picture of what you want to accomplish and then, to the best of your ability, divide up the project into phases. How many phases? That depends on the project, but generally it is someplace between two and five.

TIP

By chunking out the project into phases, you have a far better chance of not missing anything.

You know where you want to end up; identifying the two to five major phases is not arduous. Then, in a top-down manner, work within each phase to identify the events or tasks, and their associated subtasks. As you work within each phase, define everything that needs to be done; you are actually creating what is called the work breakdown structure.

THE WORK BREAKDOWN STRUCTURE

The WBS has become synonymous with a task list. The simplest form of WBS is the outline, although it can also appear as a tree diagram or other chart. Sticking with the outline, the WBS lists each task, each associated subtask, milestones, and deliverables. The WBS can be used to plot assignments and schedules and to maintain focus on the budget. The following is an example of such an outline:

1.0.0 Outline story

    11.1.0 Rough plot

        11.1.1 Establish theme

        11.1.2 Identify theme

        11.1.3 Link Story events

    11.2.0 Refine plot

        11.2.1 Create chart linking characters

        11.2.2 Identify lessons

2.0.0 Write story

    12.1.0 Lesson 1

        12.1.1 Body discovered

        12.1.2 Body identified

        12.1.3 Agent put on case

        12.1.4 Family

    12.2.0 Lesson 2

The chart shown in the following figure is particularly useful when your project has a lot of layers—that is, when many subtasks contribute to the overall accomplishment of a task, which contributes to the completion of a phase, which leads to another phase, which ultimately leads to project completion!

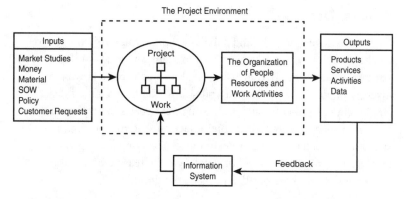

A Tree Diagram, such as the one shown here, represents another form of work breakdown structure (WBS).

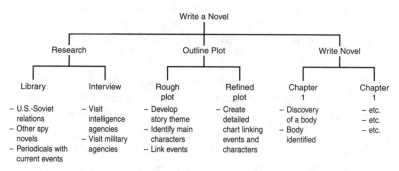

A project outline.

Keeping in mind that in many circles, deliverables are relatively synonymous with milestones, which are relatively synonymous with tasks, the WBS gives you the opportunity to break tasks into individual components. This gives you a firm grasp of what needs to be done at the lowest of levels. Hence, the WBS aids in doling out assignments, scheduling them, and budgeting for them.

DETAILS, DETAILS

How many levels of tasks and subtasks should you have? It depends on the complexity of the project. While scads and scads of details may seem overwhelming, if your work breakdown structure is well organized, you will have positioned yourself to handle even the most challenging of projects, such as hosting next year's international convention, finding a new type of fuel injection system, coordinating a statewide volunteer effort, or designing a new computer operating system. By heaping on the level of detail, you increase the probability that you will take care of all aspects of the project.

CAUTION

The potential risk of having too many subtasks is that you become hopelessly bogged down in detail and become overly focused on tasks, not outcomes!

Fortunately, as you proceed in execution, you find that some of the subtasks (and sub-subtasks) are taken care of as a result of some other action. Still, it is better to have listed more details than fewer. If you have not plotted out all that you can foresee, then once the project commences, you may be beset by all kinds of challenges because you understated the work that needs to be performed.

TIP

While the level of detail is up to you, as a general rule, the smallest of subtasks that you would list in the WBS would be synonymous with the smallest unit that you as a project manager need to keep track of.

Team-generated subtasks? Could your project management team end up making their own subwork breakdown structures to delineate their individual responsibilities, and, hence, have a greater level of detail than your WBS? The answer is yes. Ideally, you empower your staff to effectively execute delegated responsibilities. Within those assignments, there is often considerable leeway as to how the assignments are performed best.

Your good project team members may naturally gravitate toward their own mini-WBS. Often, good team members devise subtask routines that exceed what you need to preside over as project manager—unless of course the procedure is worth repeating with other project team members or on other projects in the future.

THE FUNCTIONAL WBS

In the example shown in the following figure, the WBS is divided based on separate functions. This method of plotting the WBS is particularly effective for project managers who preside over team members who may also be divided up into functional lines. In this case, the WSB gives a quick and accurate snapshot of how the project is divided up and which teams are responsible for what.

As you may readily observe, each form of WBS, outline and tree diagram, offers different benefits and has different shortcomings. For example, the outline is far more effective at conveying minute levels of detail toward the achievement of specific tasks.

CAUTION

When many subteams within an overall project team each have individual responsibilities, the outline can be a little unwieldy because it doesn't visually separate activities according to functional lines.

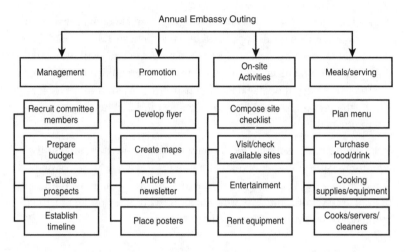

A combination tree diagram and outline WBS.

The tree diagram WBS (see the following figure) does a magnificent job of separating functional activities. Its major shortcoming is that to convey high levels of task detail, the tree diagram would be huge. It might get too big for a single piece of paper or single computer screen, and hence would have to be plotted on a large wall chart. Even then, all the tasks and subtasks of all the players in all of the functional departments would necessitate constructing a large and complex chart indeed.

Such a chart is actually a hybrid of the detailed outline and the tree diagram. Nevertheless, many project managers have resorted to this technique. By constructing both an outline and tree diagram WBS and then combining the two, however large and unwieldy the combination gets, you end up with a single document that assures the totality of the entire project.

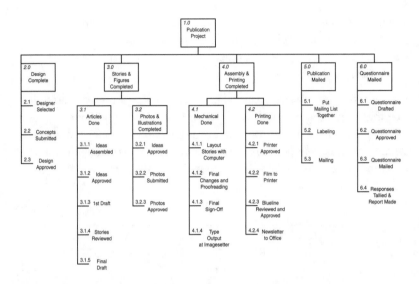

Here's an example of a segment of an outline and tree outline WBS combined.

MORE COMPLEXITY, MORE HELP

With this potential level of detail for the project you have been assigned to manage, it is important to get help when first laying out your plan. Even relatively small projects of short duration may necessitate accomplishing a variety of tasks and subtasks.

Eventually, each subtask requires an estimate of labor hours: How long will it take for somebody to complete it, and what will it cost? (See next lesson.) You will need to determine how many staff hours, staff days, staff weeks, and so on will be necessary, based on the plan that you have laid out. From there, you will run into issues concerning what staff you will be able to recruit, how many hours your staff members will be available and at what cost per hour or per day.

Preparing your WBS also gives you an indicator of what project resources may be required beyond human resources. These could include computer equipment, other tools, office or plant space and facilities, and so on.

If the tasks and subtasks that you plot out reveal that project staff will be traveling in pursuit of the desired outcome, then you have to figure in auto and airfare costs, room and board, and other associated travel expenses. If certain portions of the project will be farmed out to subcontractors or subliminal staff, there will be associated costs as well.

TIP

> Think of the WBS as your initial planning tool for meeting the project objective(s) on the way to that final, singular, sweet triumph.

WHAT SHOULD WE DELIVER?

Completing project milestones, usually conveyed in the form of a project deliverable, represents your most salient indicators that you are on target for completing the project successfully. Deliverables can take many, many forms. Many deliverables are actually related to project reporting themselves. These could include, but are not limited to, the following:

- A list of deliverables. One of your deliverables may be a compendium of all other deliverables!

- A quality assurance plan. If your team is empowered to design something that requires exact specifications, perhaps some new engineering procedure, product, or service offering, how will you assure requisite levels of quality?

- A schedule. A schedule can be a deliverable, particularly when your project has multiple phases and you are only in the first phase or the preliminary part of the first phase. It then becomes understood that as you get into the project you will have a more precise understanding of what can be delivered and when, and hence the schedule itself can become a much-anticipated deliverable.

- The overall budget, estimates, your work plan, cost benefit analysis, and other documentation can all be deliverables as well.

PLAIN ENGLISH

Cost benefit analysis   A determination of whether to proceed based on the monetary time and resources required for the proposed solution versus the desirability of the outcome(s).

Another type of deliverable has to do with acquisition and procurement. A government agency or a large contractor could empower a project manager and project management team to develop requests for proposals (RFPs), invitations to bid or requests for estimates as project deliverables. Once the proposals or bids come in, proposal evaluation procedures have to be in place.

The following are examples:

- Software evaluation plans

- Maintenance plans

- Hardware and equipment evaluation plans

- Assessment tools

The wide variety of other deliverables might include:

- Business guidelines

- Lexicon or dictionary

- Buy-versus-make analysis

- A phase out plan

- Training procedures

- Product prototype

- Implementation plans

- Reporting forms

- Application

- Product specifications

- Close out procedures

- Documentation

- Code

- Experimental Design

- Test results

- Process models

IT'S RESULTS THAT COUNT

In preparing the WBS and associated deliverables, focus on results and not activities. The plan that you lay out and eventually develop becomes the operating bible for the project team.

One project manager on a new software project requested that team-member programmers develop a certain number of lines of code per day in one phase of a project. He felt that this would be a useful indicator of the level of productivity of his individual project team members. In their efforts to be productive members of the project team, the programmers developed scads of new lines of code each day. The resulting program, however, was fraught with errors and was insufficient for completing that phase of the project. It put the overall project drastically behind schedule and behind budget.

Rather than making task and subtask assignments related to the number of lines of new code developed, the tasks and subtasks should have reflected code that accomplished a specific, observable capability. Then, project programmers would have concentrated on code efficiency and potency, as opposed to volume.

TIP

> Remember the old adage that sometimes, it's quality, not quantity, that counts.

SUPPORTING TOOLS

Undoubtedly, when laying out your plan, you will have many starts and stops, erasures, redirections, and second thoughts. If you are lucky enough to have a white board, where you can simply write down your current thoughts to have them stored to disc and printed later, then you know that this is a valuable tool indeed.

Many people simply use stick-em pads, which now come in various dimensions as large as three inches by five inches. An event or task can be confined to one stick-em note with associated subtasks on that same note or an attached note. These can then be moved around at will, as you are plotting out your plan.

Stick-em pads can even be used in combination with a white board. Simply stick them in place (or the best place you can determine at the moment). If you don't have a white board, you can also use a copying machine to take a snapshot of your current thinking.

To further ease your burden, you can use colors. These could include different colored stick-em notes, colored dots, or magic markers, flares, and highlighters. Each event or task could be a different color, or like subtasks could be a uniform color. The options are unlimited and are basically your choice.

Many project managers find it useful and convenient to use colors to track the responsibilities of individual project team members. For example, everything that Scott is responsible for will be in orange.

Many project managers also find it convenient to number tasks and subtasks.

CAUTION

> Keep it simple when numbering tasks or subtasks. You don't want to end up with outline structures such as 1–1.2.34. This ends up being more confusing than not having them numbered at all.

BOUNCE YOUR PLAN OFF OF OTHERS

After you've laid out what you feel is a comprehensive plan that will accomplish the mission, bounce it off others, even those that for one reason or another were not available to participate in its construction.

- You want people to give it a critical eye.

- You want to have them play devil's advocate.

- You want them to challenge you.

- You want them to question you as to why you went left instead of right. Maybe they immediately see something that you flat-out missed. Maybe they can suggest a way to combine several subtasks into one.

CAUTION

> You don't want to fall so in love with your WBS that you can't accept the input of others, or worse, never even see the flaws. The more involved your project is, the easier it is to miss something.

In the next lesson, we add flesh and blood to your WBS, and focus on assigning staff, timeframes, and a budget to your WBS.

THE 30-SECOND RECAP

- Regardless of how worthy your project and how brilliant your plan, keeping others informed along the way, as necessary, is your prime directive.

- Carefully scoping out the project and laying out an effective project plan minimizes the potential for surprises, indicates what needs to be done, provides clarity, and offers direction.

- The work breakdown structure (WBS) is a primary planning tool in plotting your path.

- The WBS lists each task, each associated subtask, milestones, and deliverables and can be used to plot assignments and schedules and to maintain focus on the budget.

- You don't want to fall so in love with your WBS that you can't accept the input of others and miss major flaws.

LESSON 5

Assembling Your Plan

In this lesson, you learn how to further refine your work breakdown structure (WBS), whether your labor should be part of the WBS, the importance of reintegrating project staff as the project winds down, and distinctions between the WBS and other planning tools.

THE CRITICAL PATH FOR COMPLETING THE WBS

Before a project was assigned to you, an authorizing party or committee determined that it needed to be executed. They allocated resources to the project. At the least, initially this included costs of your services. They may have also formally or informally made assignments of plant, equipment, and human resources to the project.

PLAIN ENGLISH

Critical path   The longest complete path of a project.

At some point you were summoned. You discussed the desired objective, how long the project will take, the key events in pursuit of the final objective, and whether or not the project should have distinct phases. Perhaps a feasibility study was already done. Maybe there were notes and other documents that enabled you to get a running start as to what you would be required to do. Often, your initial assignment is to define your own role and present your definition to the authorizing party or committee.

Once the decision was made to launch the project, and once you were given the formal go-ahead, laying out your plan, developing the WBS, and presentation to your superiors became the order of the day, such as that depicted in the chart shown in the figure below.

Item:	J	F	M	A	M	J	J	A	S	O	N	D
Project Launch	————											
Sponsor Approval			—									
Plan Development				—								
WBS						—						
Presentation and Approval					-							
Implementation							—————————					

Laying out the plan.

The basic activities involved to complete the WBS are as follows:

- Identify the events or task and subtasks associated with them. They are paramount to achieving the desired objective.

- Plot them using an outline, a tree diagram, or combination thereof to determine the most efficient sequence.

- Estimate the level of effort required (usually in terms of person days) and start and stop times for each task and subtask.

- Identify supporting resources and when they can be available, how long they are available, and when and how they must be returned.

- Establish a budget for the entire project, for phases if applicable, and possibly for specific events or tasks.

- Assign target dates for the completion of events or tasks known as milestones.

- Establish a roster of deliverables, many of which are presented in accordance with achieving or are analogous to milestones.

- Obtain approval of your plan from the authorizing party. See the chart in the figure below.

Item:	J	F	M	A	M	J	J	A	S	O	N	D
WBS			—									
Task			-									
Precedences			-									
Assignment				-								
Resources				-								
Budget				-								
Approval				-								

Laying out your plan.

THE CHICKEN OR THE EGG?

Preparation of your work breakdown structure (WBS) and the actual commencement of project activities is a chicken-versus-egg issue. For example, many experts advise that you first identify staffing resources and then proceed with the work breakdown structure. Following that approach, the opportunity to allocate staff as necessary comes first, followed closely by budget allocations.

CAUTION

Until you plot exactly what needs to be done, you can't allocate staff hours.

Some experts advise creating the WBS *independently* of staff allocations. First, you identify what needs to be done, and then you assemble the requisite staff resources based on the plan that you've devised. I recommend the latter, because it is a more pure approach to laying out and assembling your plan—you identify needs first and then allocate appropriate staff resources.

When does it make sense to start with the staff in mind?

- When they are all full-time

- When the project is relatively short

- When the project is labor intensive or requires a lot of expensive equipment

- When you are relatively certain that you have all the skills and experiences you need within the existing allocated staff

IS PLANNING ITSELF A TASK?

Another chicken-versus-egg issue to consider is whether or not planning itself represents a task to be included on the WBS. Experts argue that especially for large and involved projects, planning can represent a variety of tasks or events or even subtasks. Planning can even be synonymous with a project phase. For example, depending on what you're trying to achieve, the outcome of Phase I might be to develop a plan which will be crucial to the execution of Phase II.

Still, some critics argue that while planning consumes time and budgetary resources, it is not appropriate to incorporate it into the WBS. They say that the WBS and any other type of planning document merely represent the outcomes of the planning process. A plan is only considered completed when the project actually begins. Thus, the work of the project itself is separate from the plan that enabled the work to commence.

On this particular chicken-versus-egg issue, you decide whether you want to include the planning of the project as a task or event in itself or simply have it represent a prelude activity for the actual work of the project.

CAUTION

> You can't skirt chicken-versus-egg issues, as they could make a significant impact on your budget and overall project plans if you don't consider them.

WHAT ABOUT YOUR HOURS?

Should your activities and contributions to the project as project manager be listed in the work breakdown structure? Some experts say no. They argue that project management represents pure management—it is there from the beginning; it will be there at the end, and

- It is ongoing.

- It isn't a task.

- There are no milestones or deliverables attached to it.

- There are no events or activities that are dependent upon project management per se.

Those who argue that project management should be plotted in the WBS point out that although all the above may be true, the act of managing a project is a vital project input and

- It involves labor.

- It consumes resources.

- It helps to achieve outcomes.

- It is clearly a valuable resource.

- It is part of the overall budget in the form of the project manager's salary.

For these reasons, I advocate that the project management function of a project be included in the work breakdown structure.

INTERNAL RESOURCES VERSUS EXTERNAL RESOURCES

As arduous as it may seem, constructing a WBS is relatively easy when all of the resources are internal, such as your staff, equipment, and other component supporting project efforts. What about when you have to rely on external resources, such as outside vendors, consultants, part-time or supplemental staff, rented or leased facilities, and rented or leased equipment? Then the job becomes more involved.

> **CAUTION**
> External project resources are more difficult to budget, schedule, and incorporate at precisely the right time.

It can also be argued that monitoring the work of outside vendors, consultants or supplemental staff is more challenging than working with internal staff. However, external human resources who bill on an hourly or daily basis have a strong incentive to perform admirably, on time, every time.

HELPING YOUR STAFF WHEN IT'S OVER

In perfecting your WBS, have you accounted for the reintegration of your project staff back into other parts of the organization as the project winds down? This is an issue that even veteran project managers overlook. On some projects most of the staff work a uniform number of hours for most of the project. If the project veers, perhaps they work longer until the project is back on course. Sometimes, project staff work steadfastly right up to the final project outcome.

Since by design your project is a temporary engagement with a scheduled end, it is logical to assume that the fate and future activity of project team members needs to be determined before the project ends.

CAUTION

> The project manager who overlooks the concerns of project staff who are wondering about their immediate futures will find that as the project draws to a close, project staff may start to lose focus or display symptoms of divided loyalty.

Project staff justifiably are concerned about what they will be doing next, whether it is moving on to a new project, or finding their way back to their previous positions. You can't blame them, because they have their own career and own futures to be concerned with.

Abrupt changes in job status, such as working full bore on a project to a nebulous status, can be quite disconcerting to employees. Equally challenging for the project manager, however, is the situation where the brunt of the project work occurs sometimes before the actual completion date. Thus, many project staff members may be in a wind down phase—having worked more than 40 hours a week on the project at its midpoint and now perhaps spending 20 or less a week on it. They now devote the rest of the time to some other project or back at their old position.

In such cases, the project manager needs to account for issues related to diverted attention, divided loyalties, and the nagging problem of having several project staffers simply not having their "heads" in the project anymore.

TIP

The WBS needs to reflect the added measure of staff meetings, reviews, and "tête-à-têtes" that are often vital to maintain performance near the end of a project.

WHAT KINDS OF TASKS COMPRISE THE WBS?

Whether you employ an outline, tree, or combination WBS, it is useful to point out some distinction among tasks. Parallel tasks are those which can be undertaken at the same time as other tasks, without impeding the project. For example, you may have several teams working on different elements of the project that are not time or sequence related. Hence, they can all be making progress without impeding any of the other teams.

PLAIN ENGLISH

Parallel tasks   Two or more tasks that can be undertaken at the same time. This doesn't imply that they have the same starting and ending times.

Dependent tasks are those that cannot begin until something else occurs. If you are constructing a building, you first have to lay the foundation. Then, you can build the first floor, the second floor, and the third floor. Obviously, you can't start with the fifth floor and then move to the third, not in three-dimensional space as we know it.

PLAIN ENGLISH

Dependent task   A task or subtask that cannot be initiated until a predecessor task or several predecessor tasks are finished. **Predecessor task**   Task that must be completed before another task can commence.

The WBS is not the best tool for identifying the relationship between interdependent tasks. When preparing a WSB outline, you want to proceed in chronological order, much as you want to do with the tree approach. When you combine the outline and tree diagram type WBS, you end up with an extended outline describing the tasks and subtasks associated with the elements on the tree diagram. Thereafter, you can alter the position of the boxes to be in alignment with what takes place and when. Hence, parallel tasks are on the same position on the chart. As you can see in the figure below, some items, such as assignment and resource, occur at the same time.

Item:	J	F	M	A	M	J	J	A	S	O	N	D
Task A			————————									
Task B							————					
Task C						————						
Task D									———			

Adding detail to the WBS sequence.

Dependent tasks necessarily have to have staggered positions. These can be joined by the arrows that indicate the desired path of events or activities.

Milestones don't necessarily require any time or budget, as they represent the culmination of events and tasks leading up to a milestone. A milestone may or may not involve a deliverable. Nevertheless, milestones are important, particularly to project team members, because they offer a visible point of demarcation. They let team members know that the project is (or is not) proceeding according to plan. They represent a completion of sorts from which the project staff can gain new energy, focus, and direction for what comes next.

KEEPING THE BIG PICTURE IN MIND

In refining the WBS to get it to its final form it is useful to revisit the basic definition of a project as first introduced in Lesson 1, "So You're Going to Manage a Project?" The project is a venture undertaken to achieve a desired outcome, within a specific timeframe and budget. The outcome can be precisely defined and quantified. By definition, the project is temporary in nature. It usually represents a unique activity to the host organization.

The challenge of establishing an effective WBS in many ways is likened to meeting a series of constraints. For example

- Staff resources may be limited.

- The budget may be limited.

- Equipment and organizational resources may be limited.

- Crucial items on order may not arrive on time.

- Deliverables that you do prepare on time may be delayed by committees that have to go through various approval procedures.

Meanwhile, you have a project to run and can't or don't want to spend the time waiting for committee members to get their act together.

CAUTION

Even when deliverables are not the issue, there may be delays when you simply need to have a yes or no answer. Key decision makers may be unreachable or too bogged down with other issues to get back to you in what you consider to be a timely manner.

Perhaps the most troublesome and hardest to plot on your WBS is the situation where progress on your project is dependent upon the activities of some other department within your organization or the success and timely combination of some other project.

> **CAUTION**
>
> If your project is delayed for days on end because some other project team has not conveyed a key deliverable to you, you can quickly find yourself in a touchy situation.

As you assemble your plan, you have to account for delays in the time that outside parties get back to you, even though they promised that such delays would not occur!

> **TIP**
>
> From a planning standpoint, if a group is supposed to get back to you in two days, consider their turn-around time to be four days. Only then would you build into your plans a series of announcements and reminders focused on getting them to respond.

THE BIG PICTURE VERSUS ENDLESS MINUTIA

In your quest to assemble a comprehensive WBS, you may run the risk of going too far. As mentioned in Lesson 3, "What Do You Want to Accomplish?" many a project manager has made the unfortunate error of mapping out too many tasks. When you subdivide tasks into too many subtasks, the WBS could possibly become more restrictive than useful.

> **CAUTION**
>
> Some project managers have been accused, hopefully unfairly, of charting bathroom breaks for staffers.

You want to maintain control of the project and have a reasonable idea of what each project team member is doing on any given day.

In assembling your project plan, however, you don't want to go overboard. Beware if you have hundreds of items listed for each event or task area, and dozens and dozens of items scheduled each day for each staffer!

Micromanagement isn't pretty—particularly when you get into the nitty gritty details of what otherwise competent project team members should be responsible for. What is worse, micromanagement techniques often focus on the wrong issues all together.

The goal in constructing a suitable WBS and being an effective project manager is to help your staff members achieve predetermined milestones in pursuit of an overall desired project outcome. From a mathematical standpoint, the longer the lists you have, generally the more difficult it will be to complete everything on the list. In addition, the complexity of your job as project manager increases many-fold.

What number of subtasks in support of an event or task represents the optimal? Nine is probably too many and two is not enough. Someplace between three and five is probably optimal.

From Planning to Monitoring

Once the WBS is approved, your major responsibility for the duration of the project becomes that of monitoring progress. This involves a variety of responsibilities including the following:

- Keeping tabs on the course and direction of the project, noting any variation from the desired path.

- Modifying task descriptions as may become necessary as the project proceeds. Taking immediate corrective action if it appears that the project is veering while continuing to adhere to overall schedules and budgets.

- Working with team members, enhancing their understanding of their respective roles, team building, offering praise and criticism, and incorporating their feedback.

- Controlling the scope of the project, which includes making sure that the desired level of resources are expended on tasks and subtasks according to plan.

- Ensuring that roadblocks and barriers are effectively overcome and that you don't end up winning some battles at the cost of losing the war—sometimes you can expend too much effort in one area and end up leaving yourself in a weakened position someplace else.

- Maintaining effective relationships with the authorizing party and stakeholders, keeping them informed, maintaining a "no surprises" type of approach, and incorporating their feedback.

Lesson 6, "Keeping Your Eye on the Budget," examines the importance of expending resources carefully including dealing with budgetary constraints, equipment constraints, and other potential roadblocks. Thereafter, in Lesson 7, "Gantt Charts," Lesson 8, "PERT/CPM Charts," and Lessons 10, "Choosing Project Management Software," and 11, "A Sampling of Popular Programs," we dicuss how to manage more involved projects.

THE 30-SECOND RECAP

- In assembling your WBS, there are several chicken-versus-egg issues that must be resolved, such as whether to plot your own activities as a project manager and whether to include planning itself as a task.

- Project managers have an easier time maintaining control of internal resources including staff, equipment, and facilities, than managing external resources including consultants, rented equipment, and leased facilities.

- Your WBS needs to reflect realistic delays in getting feedback from committees following their reception of your scheduled deliverables.

- Once you nail the WBS, you shift from a planning to a monitoring mode.

LESSON 6
Keeping Your Eye on the Budget

In this lesson, you learn how optimism gets in the way of controlling expenses, effective approaches to budgeting, how to combine top-down and bottom-up budgeting techniques, and the importance of building in slack.

MONEY STILL DOESN'T GROW ON TREES

One of the primary responsibilities that you have as project manager is to keep close reins on the budget. Your organization or whoever is funding the project enjoys hearing about cost overruns about as much as having a root canal.

Too often the monetary resources allocated to a project (perhaps even before you stepped aboard) have been underestimated. Why? Because of the irrational exuberance that the authorizing party or stakeholder may have as to what can be achieved at what cost. This is not to say that project managers don't have their own hand in underestimating cost.

The project manager often is charged with determining the project budget, as opposed to being handed some figure from above. In such cases, it always pays to estimate on the high side. This is true for many reasons:

- In most organizations, no matter how much you ask for, *you can count on not getting it all.*

TIP

> You might as well ask for slightly more than your best calculations indicate, thereby increasing the probability of getting close to the amount you actually seek.

- No matter how precise your calculations, how much slack you allow, or what kind of contingencies you have considered, chances are your estimate is still low.

PLAIN ENGLISH

> **Slack**   Margin or extra room to accommodate anticipated potential short falls in planning.

PLAIN ENGLISH

> **Murphy's Law**   The age-old axiom stating that if something can go wrong, it will go wrong.
> **Parkinson's Law**   Work expands so as to fill the time allotted for its completion.

- In ever-changing business, social, and technological environments, no one has a lock on the future even three months out, let alone three years out. You simply have to build into your budget extra margins beyond those that seem initially commensurate with the overall level of work to be performed and outcome to be achieved.

Is it foolhardy to prepare a budget that merely reflects the best computation as to what the sum ought to be? Probably.

Experience Pays

Your level of experience as a project manager plays a big part in your ability to understand the real monetary costs in conducting the project. For example, a highly skilled laborer may be able to work wonders with less than top-of-the-line equipment, whereas an entry-level laborer is likely to be less productive in the same situation.

Distorted Expectations

Another problem is related to your own competence. The more competent you are as a project manager and as a career professional in general, the greater the tendency for you to underestimate the time necessary for project staff members to complete a job. You tend to envision the completion of a job through the eyes of your own level of competency. Even if you discount for newly-hired and inexperienced staff, you still tend to regard jobs in the way that you might have tackled them when you were newly hired. Hence, you end up underestimating the time required to complete the job with the staff that you *do have* by 5, 10, 15 percent or more.

The preceding phenomenon has a corollary in professional sports, particularly in NBA basketball. Many of the superstars who went on to become head coach failed miserably because they could not budget for the lower competency levels of players on their current roster. Such coaches thought back to their own days and what they were able to achieve, perhaps even thought of competent teammates and competent players from other teams. When coaching their current team, they couldn't shake their preconceived notion of what a player was supposed to be able to do, the rate at which a player learned, and the skill level that the player could acquire.

Hidden Costs

An experienced project manager also knows that any time you rely on external sources to proceed on a project, such as subcontractors, there are hidden costs involved. The subcontractor may work for a flat fee or lump sum amount, and, if so, it's easy to pinpoint that figure and plug it into the overall budget. However, what about your time and effort, or project team members' time and effort, in carefully preparing guidelines for subcontractors, working with them to ensure smooth operation, and consuming time in extra meetings, phone calls, and e-mails? What about the extra reporting and other administrative tasks associated with working with outside vendors? Such factors ultimately impact the budget.

CAUTION

> The cumulative impact of underestimating time can quickly put your project in jeopardy. Even if you apply a safety margin to your estimate, the level of safety margin is applied through the eyes of your own personal competency. Hence, you need to get help when preparing the budget.

CRISES WILL HAPPEN

The experienced project manager expects that one or more crises will occur in the course of the project. The inexperienced project manager may have been forewarned, but still is unprepared. Even experienced project managers know that sometimes you reach a point of desperation in the project—you must have something done by a certain time and need to move heaven and earth to do it. You may have to pay exorbitant short-term costs to procure a vital resource, work around the clock, plead for added help, make thinly veiled threats, or scramble like a rabbit in the brush to keep the project on time. All such instances have a potentially dramatic effect on the budget.

TRADITIONAL APPROACHES TO BUDGETING

If you're managing a project that remotely resembles anything else anyone has managed in your organization, you may be able to extract some clues as to how to prepare a real-world budget for your project. Obviously, you never want to merely lift the cost figures from one project and apply it to yours.

> **TIP**
>
> There may be cost elements of a previous project that are akin to some elements of your project, so that's as good a place to start as any.

Many industries have already codified cost elements associated with various jobs. Printers have elaborate cost estimate sheets. Their estimators can plug in the particulars of a customer's request and quickly yield a cost estimate for the customer. With the many variables involved in estimating the cost of a printing job, however, the estimator can end up underestimating the true costs and hence diminish his profit.

In construction, the cost estimator has comparable tools for the construction industry. The estimator may know the costs for each 2' by 4', brick, cinder block, and glass panel.

Still, you hear stories about printing jobs that ended up costing 50 percent or more of the original estimate, of companies taking a bath on projects because the final costs were so out of whack with reality. Particularly in civic and civil engineering projects, cost overruns in the millions of dollars make for regular news features in every community. What is going on here? Why would experienced organizations that have the most sophisticated cost estimating software, and undoubtedly have performed hundreds of jobs for clients and customers be off the mark so often and sometimes so wildly? It all comes down to the skill of the person doing the budget estimate, the assumptions he or she relies upon, and the approach he or she takes.

TIP

> By knowing the dimensions of the building, the number of floors, and all the other attributes via project blueprints to the best of his ability, the experienced estimator determines the overall cost of the construction project.

TRADITIONAL MEASURES

Let's discuss some traditional measures for preparing a budget, followed by a look at the cost estimation traps that you don't want to fall into.

TOP-DOWN BUDGETING

Using this approach, a project manager surveys the authorizing party or committee, stakeholders, and certainly top and middle managers where relevant. The project manager would also conduct a massive hunt for all previous cost data on projects of a remotely similar nature. He would then compile the costs associated with each phase (if the project is divided into phases), specific events or tasks, or even subtasks.

To further hedge his bet, he might even enroll project management staff if they have been identified in advance, and get their estimates of the time (and hence cost) for specific tasks and subtasks. He would then refine his own estimates, which now may be somewhat higher than the figure his peers may have arrived at. In any case, he would represent his data to the authorizing party.

TIP

> More often than not, the wise project manager lobbies for a larger budget than the authorizing party feels is necessary.

Even if the project manager ends up yielding to the wishes of the authorizing party (and when hasn't this happened?) and accepts a lower budget figure, there are some safeguards built into the top-down budgeting approach. The judgments of senior, top-level, highly experienced executives and managers likely already factor in budgetary safety margins and contingencies.

In addition, the project manager may be one project manager of many calling on the top manager or executive. Hence, the amount allocated for his budget is probably in alignment and consistent with the overall needs of the department, division, or entire organization. A highly persuasive project manager may be able to lobby for a few percent more in funding, but probably not much more unless there are extraordinary circumstances.

BOTTOM-UP BUDGETING

As the name implies, this approach to budgeting takes the reverse course. After constructing work breakdown structure, the project manager consults with project staff members (presumably pre-identified) who offer highly detailed estimates of the budget required for each task and subtask at every step along the way. In fact, the project manager routinely surveys the staff once the project begins to continue to formulate the bottom-up budget, which he then submits to the higher-ups. The project manager keeps a sharp eye on trends—possibly on a daily basis, more likely on a weekly or biweekly basis, and certainly between one task and another.

As project team members proceed up the learning curve, they are often able to achieve operating efficiencies that enable the overall project team to proceed on some aspects of the project with much greater productivity, and hence lower costs. This isn't to say that the project won't hit a snag or is otherwise immune to the potential cost overruns as discussed throughout this lesson.

The bottom-up budgeting approach holds great potential but also carries great risk. Potentially, a highly detailed, reasonably accurate compilation of costs can be achieved using this method. The danger is that if the project manager does not include all cost elements of the project, then the cost estimate understandably can be off by a wide margin.

> **CAUTION**
>
> In *Project Management*, Meredith and Mantel state, "It is far more difficult to develop a complete list of tasks when constructing that list from the bottom up than from the top down."

In addition, if project management staff suspects that top management is on the lookout to cut budgets, then they may resort to overstating their case. This results in the project manager presenting a sum to the higher-ups that is larger than would otherwise be derived. In turn, the potential for the project budget being whittled away increases. What a process!

Nevertheless, as more and more organizations request that their project managers engage in project management, it makes sense to regularly solicit the input from those who are actually doing the work. Line workers in any industry have a first person, hands on connection to what is occurring—whereas staff usually are somewhat distant observers often relying on compiled information.

When project staff gets to participate in the preparation of budgets, if those budgets are cut, at least they had some role in the process and hence "will accept the result with a minimum of grumbling," according to Meredith and Mantel. "Involvement is also a good managerial training technique, giving junior managers valuable experience in budget preparation as well as the knowledge of the operations required to generate a budget."

TOP-DOWN AND BOTTOM-UP BUDGETING

Perhaps the most effective approach combines the two budgeting techniques discussed thus far. It involves gathering all the data and input from top executives and then soliciting input from project management staff and adjusting estimates accordingly.

CAUTION

Despite some wonderful benefits, most organizations and most projects do not rely upon bottom-up budgeting. Top managers are reluctant to relinquish control of one of their chief sources of power—allocating monies—and sometimes mistrust subordinates who they may believe routinely overstate project needs.

Regardless of the approach, one needs to account for the ever-present disparity between actual hours on the job and actual hours worked. No project staff person working an eight-hour day offers eight hours of unwavering productivity. There are breaks, timeouts, lapses, unwarranted phone calls, Internet searches, and who knows what else going on. Hence, you may wish to apply a 10 percent to 15 percent increase in the estimates submitted by project management staff in regard to the amount of time it will take them to accomplish tasks and subtasks.

If a particular task initially was determined to cost $1,000 (the worker's hourly rate times the number of hours), you would then allocate $1,100 or $1,150 dollars to more closely reflect the true costs to the organization. Taking the midpoint of your calculation, $1,135 dollars, you would plug that into the figures you then present back to top management.

Reverting back and forth between top management and line workers in the quest to pinpoint accurate costs is not a rare phenomenon among project managers. In many respects, budget approvals require a series of periodic authorizations. Depending upon how your organization views project management and earlier protocols established, your project may only proceed based on a constant flow of budgetary checks and balances. The following table is one example of a project budget with actual and budgeted amounts recorded.

Project Budgeting

	Actual Variance	Budget Percent
Corporate-Income Statement		
Revenue		
30 Management fees		
91 Prtnsp reimb— property mgmt	410.00 188.00	222.00 119.0
92 Prtnsp reimb— owner acquisition	.00 750.00–	750.00 .0
93 Prtnsp reimb—rehab	.00	.00
94 Other income	.00	.00
95 Reimbursements—others	.00	.00
Total revenue	410.00 562.00–	972.00 74.3
Operating expenses		
Payroll & P/R benefits		
11 Salaries	425.75 57.25	583.00 85.0

12 Payroll taxes	789.88	458.00
	668.12	51.7
13 Group ins & med reimb	407.45	40.00
	387.45–	135.3
15 Workmens compensation	43.04	43.00
	.04–	100.0
16 Staff apartments	.00	.00
17 Bonus	.00	.00
Total payroll & P/R benefits	1668.12	1124.00
	457.88	83.5

SYSTEMATIC BUDGETING PROBLEMS

When you consider all the potential costs associated with a task or subtask, it's easy to understand why some costs may not be budgeted accurately.

Suppose you are charged with managing a project to design some new proprietary software system that will be one of the leading products for your company. Consider the following:

- There will be a variety of system development costs including defining system requirements, designing the system, designing infrastructure, coding, unit testing, networking, and integrating, as well as documentation, training materials, possibly consulting costs, possibly licenses, and fees.

- Maybe you have staff costs as well to identify, configure, and purchase hardware, to install it, and to maintain it. Similar staff costs may accrue to acquiring software.

- There could be staff travel, transportation, hotel and meal expense, conference room and equipment fees, fees for coffee service, snacks, and other refreshments.

- There are costs involved in having top management, outside vendors, and clients and customers attend briefings.

- There could be costs associated with testing and refinement, operations, maintenance, refinement, debugging, beta testing, surveying, and compiling data.

CAUTION

Little or no prior data may be available that the project manager can draw upon to help estimate such a multifaceted project. Budgets from previous projects may serve to confuse and complicate issues, rather than clarify and simplify them.

In particular, look out for these estimation *faux pas*:

- Inexperienced estimators who don't follow any consistent methodology in preparing estimates overlook some cost items entirely, or tend to be too optimistic about what is needed to do the job.

- If you are managing a project that has a direct payoff for a specific client, you have to consider that your organization had to bid very tightly against considerable competition. Perhaps they bid too tightly to get the job done (low-balled to win a contract award). It now becomes your responsibility to work within these constraints. In such cases, you find yourself trying to trim costs every step of the way, even when there is nothing left to trim.

  Sometimes organizations intentionally bid on projects they know will be money losers. They do this in the hopes that it will establish a relationship with the customer that will lead to other, more lucrative projects. This is little solace for you if you are the one trying to grind out every ounce of productivity you can from an already overworked project staff or having to use plants and equipment to the max.

- In some organizations the most careful and comprehensive project budgets end up being slashed by some senior managers or executives who are operating based on some agenda to which you are not privy. In his book *The New Project Management*, author J.D. Frame says, "Political meddling in cost and schedule estimating is an everyday occurrence in some organizations." The best antidote against such meddling, says the author, is "the establishment of objective, clearly defined procedures for project selection …" which should be set up so that no one, "no matter how powerful, can unilaterally impose their will on the selection process."

The issues raised in this lesson point to the ever present need for project managers to build an appropriate degree of slack into their estimates. This is not to say that you are being dishonest or disloyal to your organization, but rather acknowledging the ruthless rules of project management reality—you hardly ever get the funds you need, and even then, stuff happens!

THE 30-SECOND RECAP

- Because of irrational exuberance, too often the monetary resources allocated to a project (perhaps even before you stepped aboard) have been underestimated.

- In most organizations, no matter how much you ask for, *you can count on not getting it all.*

- Perhaps the most effective approach to budgeting combines the top-down and bottom-up techniques.

- Build an appropriate degree of slack into your estimates!

LESSON 7
Gantt Charts

In this lesson, you learn what a Gantt chart is, why it is so useful in project management, variations you can devise, and how to use Gantt charts to keep your project on schedule.

CHART YOUR PROGRESS

Henry L. Gantt, for whom the Gantt chart is named, was employed at the Aberdeen Proving Grounds (part of what is now the U.S. Department of Defense—then called the War Department) in Aberdeen, Maryland—as an ordinance engineer during the First World War. Although nearly a century has passed, the Gantt chart remains widely recognized as a fundamental, highly applicable tool for project managers everywhere. A Gantt chart enables you to view start and stop times easily for project tasks and subtasks.

> **TIP**
>
> Gantt charts are derived from your work breakdown structure (WBS).

If you use an outline for your WBS, the Gantt depicts each of the tasks and subtasks in chronological order. For tasks that begin at the same time and run concurrently, the Gantt chart is a highly convenient tool. However, over-lapping tasks and subtasks can easily be depicted on the Gantt chart as well.

A WBS is created from tree diagrams, which also lend themselves to depiction on a Gantt chart—although the process is a bit tricky when it comes to determining overall project sequence and start and stop times. (More on converting tree diagrams to critical path analysis in Lesson 8, "PERT/CPM Charts.")

Two basic forms of Gantt charts are depicted here. The following chart uses bars extending from left to right along the horizontal axis to denote starting and ending times for events or activities. Greater detail could be added if you wish to add subtasks. Color-coding allows you to pinpoint which project workers are handling which tasks and sub-tasks. The chart shown in the following figure offers a simple plan for depicting the planned sequence of events versus the actual (the shaded bars). It is a rare project indeed where the brunt of the planned events or tasks are closely mirrored by the actual performance and completion of them:

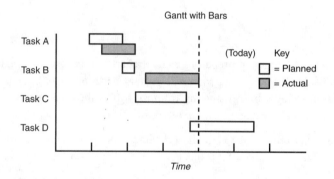

A Gantt chart with bars.

The chart shown in the next figure is merely an alternative to the previous one. Rather than using bars to depict start and stop times and shaded bars to depict actual performance versus planned performance, this chart uses

- Unshaded triangles pointing up to depict plan start time
- Unshaded triangles pointing down to depict plan end time

- Shaded triangles pointing up to depict actual start time
- Shaded triangles pointing down to depict actual completion time

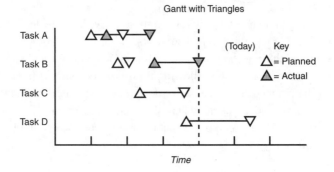

Gantt with Triangles

Time

A Gantt chart with triangles.

One of the advantages of preparing a Gantt chart in this format is that tasks and subtasks, and planned versus actual timeframes can be depicted on a single line emanating from the left of the chart, extending out along the horizontal axis to the right.

The two variations of the Gantt chart depicted above (there are many others), offer a snapshot of a project's progress based on timeframes.

In the first figure, although Task 1 didn't start on time, its duration was roughly equal to the original planned time.

In Task 2, however, the start time was not only delayed, but the actual completion time for the task was far greater than originally planned. This could signal potential budgetary problems or human resource bottlenecks here or at other points as the project progresses.

If the start of Task 3 is not dependent upon the results of Task 2, then the manager can make a decision to initiate Task 3 as scheduled or even earlier, since delays in starting Task 2 may indicate the availability of idle resources.

If Task 3, however, *is* dependent upon the completion of Task 2, or at least the brunt of it, then the project manager may have no alternative but to have Task 3 start late as well. You can see that the delays in Task 1 and Task 2 may have a cascading effect which puts all project activities behind schedule unless the project manager is able to reallocate resources so as to pick up the slack where possible.

VARIATIONS ON A THEME

The Gantt chart in the following figure for a construction project depicts an eight-week period that includes four events, three of which are actual tasks and one representing completion of the project. Each of the three tasks has between four and six subtasks. Virtually all project activity is dependent upon maintaining the sequence of events as depicted.

The coding at the bottom of the chart indicates critical and noncritical progress related and management critical events.

- Scheduled start and stop times for the duration of tasks are earmarked by solid, downward-pointing triangles emanating from the start and end of progress bars.

- Milestones are depicted by dark diamonds.

- More detail could be added to this chart in the form of other kinds of lines and symbols.

The project manager for this chart probably found this level of coding to be useful and convenient for his purposes.

TIP

> Each of the three Gantt charts depicted thus far represent plainly evident ways of illustrating overall project status while including the status of each task. Thus, they serve as valuable tools for keeping project team members abreast of activities, as well as the authorizing party, committees, top managers and executives, and other stakeholders.

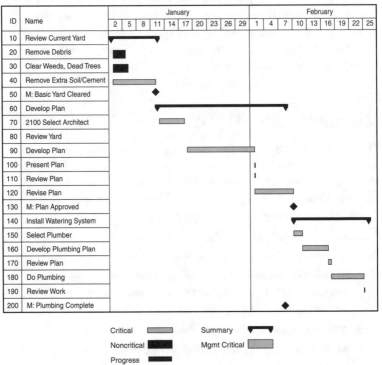

A Gantt chart for sequential construction.

EMBELLISHMENTS OFFER DETAIL

The more tasks involved in your project and the more important the sequence between tasks, the greater your propensity to embellish your Gantt chart. The chart in the next figure contains some highly useful added columns.

Gantt with Multiple Predecessors

ID	Name	Duration (Days)	Predecessors	Jan	Feb	Mar	Apr
21	Project Mgmt.	4					
22	Needs Analysis	11					
23	Specifications	7	22				
24	Select Server	8	23				
25	Select Software	14	23				
26	Select Cables	5	24				
27	Purchasing	4	25, 26				
28	Manuals	15	7				
29	Wire Offices	23	7				
30	Set Up Server	5	7				
31	Develop Training	16	8				
32	Install Software	5	10				
33	Connect Network	5	9, 12				
34	Train Users	10	11, 13				
35	Test/Debug	15	13				
36	Acceptance	6	14, 15				

Critical ■■■■   Noncritical ▨▨▨

A Gantt chart with multiple predecessors.

- Column 3,"duration," lists how many days each task is scheduled to take.

- Column 4, "predecessors," identifies what needs to be completed before this task can be initiated.

Often the previous task needs to be completed, but this isn't always the case:

- For the purchasing Task 7, both Tasks 5 and 6 need to be complete.

- For Tasks 8, 9, and 10, only Task 7 needs to be complete, as Tasks 8, 9, and 10 all start at the same time.

- For Task 12, "install software," Task 10 needs to be complete, but Task 11, which is scheduled to start after, does not.

You may wonder, "Why not switch Tasks 11 and 12 in the Gantt chart?" The answer is that Task 11, "developed training," follows directly from the completion of Task 8, "manuals"—whereas Task 12, "install software," directly follows from the completion of Task 10, "set up server." They are listed in sequence on the Gantt chart *based on what they follow, not based on when they start.*

One of the benefits of listing the task duration in days is that it also gives you a strong indicator of required levels of staff support. In the simplest example, if all staff members have the same capability, and a ten-day project requires one staff person per day, you could simply add the total number of days in the duration column and get a total number of staff days necessary for the project.

CAUTION

Leave yourself (as project manager) *out* of the duration computation, because you are fully involved in management and not engaged in any individual task.

The challenge gets more complex when two, three, four, or more staff people are needed per task for each day of a task's duration or, when varying numbers of staff people are needed per task, per day. It gets complicated further if the skill levels of project staff vary widely.

TIP

Project management software solves many issues related to multiple resource complexity. First, however, you have to understand the basics with paper and pencil, just as you have to learn the fundamentals of math on your own before being able to successfully use a calculator.

Getting a Project Back on Track

Whenever you find yourself falling behind in one area, you have to make managerial decisions as to how you will compensate to keep the overall project on track. This involves a shuffling of resources, altering the scope of selected tasks or subtasks, or changing sequence of tasks. Let's visit each of these.

- **Reallocating Resources**   It happens to the best of project managers. You launch into a task, and soon enough you find yourself under-resourced. You didn't know that a particular task or subtask was going to be so challenging. If it's critical to the overall project, it makes sense to borrow resources from other task areas.

- **Reducing the Level of Effort on Tasks or Subtasks**   Just as you discovered that some tasks clearly mandate greater staff resources, you may also find tasks and subtasks that could be completed with *less* effort than you originally budgeted. Perhaps some subtasks can be combined, or skipped all together. For example, if you're doing survey work, perhaps you can get a reasonable result with eight questions instead of 10. Perhaps you can reduce the total number of interviews by 10 percent.

- **Altering the Task Sequence**   Another possibility when faced with roadblocks is to change the sequence of tasks or subtasks. Can you substitute easier tasks for more challenging ones until some of your other staff resources are free? Perhaps you can devise a sequence that enables some of your more experienced staff members to manage multiple tasks for a brief duration.

Thinking Ahead

The Gantt chart is a useful device for engaging in "what-if" questions. As you look at the sequence of events, their duration, and the number of allotted staff days, sometimes you see opportunities to make shifts in advance of the need. Such shifts may help things to run more smoothly down the road.

> **TIP**
>
> If you find that the first several tasks or subtasks to your project are already falling behind, a Gantt chart can help you identify where else this may happen given your operating experience. Hence, you can begin crafting alternative scenarios—alternative Gantt charts that may prove to be more effective for managing the duration of the project.

You may have the pleasant experience of having tasks and subtasks completed in far less time than you had originally plotted. So, use the Gantt chart to reschedule subsequent events, moving them up and taking advantage of the temporary gains that have already been realized.

In summary, the ease of preparation, use, alteration, and sheer versatility of Gantt charts makes them a marvelous tool for both managing your project and depicting your progress to others.

The 30-Second Recap

- The Gantt chart is widely recognized as a fundamental, highly applicable tool for project managers to enable one to easily view start and stop times for project tasks and subtasks.

- The more tasks involved in your project and the more important the sequence between tasks, the greater your propensity and desire to embellish your Gantt chart.

- The Gantt chart helps answer "what-if" questions when you see opportunities to make shifts in advance of the need.

LESSON 8
PERT/CPM Charts

In this lesson, you learn why projects get increasingly complex, the fundamentals of PERT and CPM charts, why PERT and CPM charts are inexorably linked, and how to use the critical path method to conserve resources.

PROJECTS CAN GET COMPLEX

Complexity happens more often than we care for it to happen. Take the case where you are managing a two- or three-person team. If it is you and another person, you have only one other connection between the two of you. With three people on a project you have three connections. One between you and person A, another between you and person B, and one between person A and B (see the figure below). Oh, if only things stayed that simple.

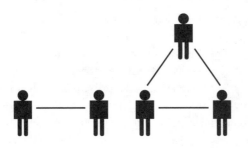

Two people, one connection and three people, three connections.

When there are four people on a project there are six connections, and with five people, there are ten connections, as shown in the following figure.

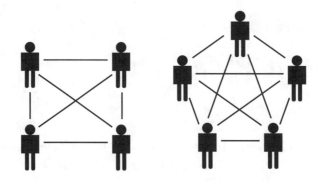

Four people, six connections and five people, ten connections.

When there are six people on a project there are 15 interpersonal connections, and when there are seven people on a project there are 21. This simple mathematical algorithm reveals that on a project beyond four or five people, the number of interconnections grows rapidly and can even become unwieldy. Now suppose that you have a vital piece of equipment that needs to be shared among several of your project staff. Throw in some other resource constraints as to when they can use that piece of equipment, when the equipment needs to be maintained, and the probability of it being unavailable for repair time.

Now, add a second resource, such as another piece of equipment, access to a database, or reliance upon a survey in process. Pretty quickly, with a lot of people on your project team, and with time, money, or resource constraints, effective management can get very involved in a hurry. Throw in some tasks that are dependent upon completion of previous tasks and you have the recipe for bottlenecks, roadblocks, and potentially massive project inefficiencies.

TIP

Complexity as project resources grow is not anybody's fault. It is just the nature of numbers, interconnectedness, restraints, and dependencies.

The Gantt chart, discussed in Lesson 7, is a valuable tool particularly for projects with a small number of project team members, the project end approaching, and few project constraints. For larger, longer-term projects involving many people, resources, and constraints, project managers need more sophisticated tools for maintaining control.

PLAIN ENGLISH

Project constraint   A critical project element such as money, time, or human resources, which frequently turns out to be in short supply.

ENTER THE PERT AND CPM

The Program Evaluation and Review Technique, widely referred to and hereafter exclusively referred to as PERT, offers a degree of control that simply becomes essential for many projects. Using PERT, a project manager can identify a task or set of tasks that represent a defined sequence crucial to project success.

A second project management technique whose fundamental approach is close to PERT is called the Critical Path Method, or CPM. The critical path in a project is the one that takes the longest to complete. So, the critical path never has any slack. If you fall behind along the critical path, the whole project falls behind schedule.

TIP

Even if you never have to engage in PERT/CPM analysis, it's good to know the fundamentals.

PERT was developed by Booz—Allan Hamilton and the Lockheed Corporation in participation with the U.S. Navy on their Polaris Missile/Submarine project back in 1958. CPM was developed by

Dupont Incorporated around the same time. While each approach has individual features, for our purposes they are close enough to treat them as virtually one and the same, so hereafter, we will refer to PERT/CPM as a unified approach to project management.

PERT/CPM enables a project manager to address issues such as

- What will happen during the project if a noncritical task slips by two weeks?

- What will happen if a critical task slips by a few days and ends up starting at the same time as another critical task?

- If I have to keep project staff on one task for an extra three days, how will it impact all remaining tasks?

A SHORT COURSE

By definition, the critical path always represents that path that takes the most time to complete. So, the critical path never contains any slack. Delays along the critical path impact the entire project. Tasks not on the critical path, by definition, always have some slack in their completion time.

CAUTION Those assigned to noncritical path tasks don't have to work quite as diligently as those on the critical path. If they are not careful, however, their total duration can exceed that of the critical paths, and thus they could put the project behind as well.

Keeping in mind that this is the *10-Minute Guide to Project Management* and not a 480-page tome, let's look at how you could use PERT/CPM to manage a simple project. We'll keep it to 10 events or tasks, including a start and an end, so only eight tasks require attention. There will only be two people on this project, you and a friend.

1. Create a work breakdown structure for the project. The following figure will serve as our example:

	Task	Duration (mins.)	
	Word-Breakdown Structure for an Outing		
1.	Start	6	
2.	Make drinks	30	Bill
3.	Prepare sandwiches	20	Erika
4.	Prepare fruit	4	Erika
5.	Prepare basket	4	Erika
6.	Gather blankets	4	Bill
7.	Gather sports gear	6	Erika
8.	Load car	8	Bill
9.	Get gas	12	Bill
10.	Drive to outing	40	Erika
11.	End	0	

Work breakdown structure (WBS).

In this example, the path that takes the most time is Task 10, the drive to the outing site.

2. Using the information in the WBS, create a flow chart such as that depicted in the next figure. Notice that in this flow chart some tasks can occur simultaneously. The tasks that Bill works on are depicted above, and the tasks Erika works on are depicted below.

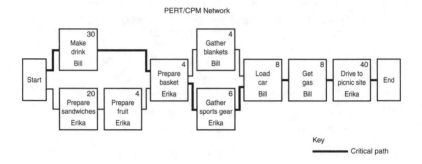

PERT/CPM Network

PERT/CPM network.

The relationships between the boxes are indicated with dark or fine lines. For example, "prepare desert" and "prepare casserole" are connected by a thin line. Bill's task "make drinks" connects to "load up food basket" with a thick line, which we will get to in a moment.

Both Bill's and Erika's tasks lead to "fill up food basket."

3. Because "make drinks" takes 30 minutes and Erika's tasks take 20 minutes and four minutes respectively, "make drinks" represents the critical path in this project—hence, the black line between Bill's first and second activity.

Erika's path has six minutes of slack built in. If she starts a few minutes late or takes a minute or two between tasks, she will still finish before Bill, as long as her total slack does not exceed six minutes. Conceivably, she could take her time on each project, adding a minute or two to each and still finish before Bill, and if her slack equals six minutes, she will finish at the same time as Bill.

4. The critical path for the entire project as depicted above can be traced by

1. Noting which tasks occur simultaneously.

2. Noting which ones take longer.

3. Routing the critical path through them.

4. Summing the entire length of the critical path.

In the preceding case, the entire project would take 100 minutes. It all sounds straightforward so far, doesn't it?

5. For this or any other type of project, look at the earliest times that critical tasks need to start. Then determine the earliest times that non-critical paths could start. Column 2 of the next figure indicates the earliest start times for all of Bill's and Erika's individual, as well as combined tasks.

Task	Early Start	Late Start	Slack
Make drinks	0	0	0
Prepare sandwiches	0	6	6
Prepare fruit	20	26	6
Prepare basket	30	30	0
Gather blankets	34	36	2
Gather sports gear	34	34	0
Load car	40	40	0
Get gas	48	48	0
Drive to outing	60	60	0

Roster of events, with start, stop, and slack time.

Column 3 shows the latest start times for Tasks 2, 3, and 6, the first two handled by Erika, and the latter handled by Bill. The total slack time for Tasks 2, 3, and 6 respectively are six, six, and two minutes as depicted in Column 4.

PLAIN ENGLISH

Slack time   The time interval in which you have leeway as to when a particular task needs to be completed.
Total slack time   The cumulative sum of time that various tasks can be delayed without delaying the completion of a project.

In calculating the latest start times, you simply work from right to left. Focusing on the critical path, if the overall project takes 100 minutes, the latest start time for the last project ("drive to the family outing site") occurs at the 60th minute. This is derived by subtracting 40 minutes of driving from 100 total project minutes.

In a similar fashion, "filling up the tank" and "cleaning the car windows" should commence by the 48th minute. The drive begins at the 60th minute and the service station stop lasts twelve minutes. Hence, 60 minus 12 is 48. All the other values can be computed similarly.

6. The computation for determining the latest start times for non-critical times also proceeds from right to left, similar to that described above. A slack time is simply computed by subtracting the earliest determined start times from the latest possible start times. Said alternatively, simply subtract the values in Column 2 from the values in Column 3 and the resulting value in Column 4 represents your slack time.

TIP

Notice that there is only slack time when both project team members are simultaneously engaged in individual projects. When both work on the same project, there is no slack time—in this example joint project activities are on the critical path.

WHAT IF THINGS CHANGE?

By chance, if Bill finishes Task 2 "making the drinks" in less than 30 minutes and Erika has done her job as scheduled, up to six minutes could be reduced on the overall project critical path. If Erika starts at the earliest times indicated, works diligently, and finishes at the 24th minute mark as planned, conceivably, she could help with some of Bill's subtasks that lead to the successful completion of Task 2. It may save a few minutes off the total project time.

Just the reverse may happen, however. In her attempt to help Bill, she may end up spilling something, mixing the wrong ingredient, or otherwise causing a delay. If so, you would add back minutes to the critical path determination commensurate to the length of the delay caused.

Because all tasks' durations represent estimates, and very few will go according to plan, the overall project time may vary widely from what Bill and Erika first estimated. They may save one to two minutes on Tasks 5, 8, and 9. Conversely, there may be a traffic build up this fine Saturday morning, and instead of 40 minutes, the trip takes an extra 10.

TIP

> While time saved sometimes compensates for time lost, on many projects, invariably some tasks throw the project manager for a loop, and require 20 percent to 50 percent more time than budgeted. The project manager who has consulted with others (see Lessons 4, "Laying Out Your Plan," and 5, "Assembling Your Plan") and engaged in both top-down and bottom-up types of planning hopefully can avoid such wide variances. Don't count on it.

I FEEL THE NEED, THE NEED FOR SPEED

Along the critical path, adding more resources to the mix potentially shortens the overall timeframe. If a friend helps Bill and Erika load up the car, a minute may be saved. This is not a dramatic example, but think about the effect of having one person help another move from one apartment to another. The addition of a second worker yields dramatic time savings, especially for bulky, oblong, or heavy items that one person could not easily handle.

When additional resources are allocated for a particular task, this is called crashing (a funny name for a beneficial phenomenon). Crash time represents the least amount of time it would take to accomplish a task or subtask with unlimited resources with which to approach the task—all the equipment or all the money you could ask for.

In *Project Management*, authors Meredith and Mantel estimate that less than 10 percent of the total activities on real world projects actually represent critical activities. Interestingly, most models and most discussions of PERT/CPM depict projects where critical activities outnumber/outweigh noncritical activities!

Most tasks have several subtasks associated with them. So the PERT/CPM network depicted in 8B offers only a broad-brush look at a rather simple project. Examining Task 1 further, suppose that one of the subtasks involved is to add sugar. As Bill mixes up the drinks he puts in a tablespoon of sugar, then he tastes the drink. Is it sweet enough? His answer is subjective, but nevertheless it will be *yes* or *no*.

If it is *no* then he has a new subtask: adding more sugar. He then makes the taste test again and eventually concludes that the sweetness is just right. At that point, he proceeds onto packing up the drinks. This activity can be depicted by the flow chart in the following figure.

If we were to incorporate the simple loop we have created in the "make drinks" flow chart (see the preceding figure) into the overall PERT/CPM chart depicted earlier in this lesson, we would have additional boxes with additional lines with additional arrows emulating from Task 1, "make drinks," thus complicating our chart.

Likewise, all other tasks may have subtasks associated with them that involve *yes* and *no* questions and repeat loops until a condition is satisfied, hence, the introduction of more delays and the increasing complexity of our PERT/CPM diagram.

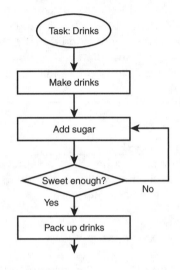

Flow chart of "make drinks" event.

LET'S NETWORK

A complete depiction of tasks and subtasks expanding on the chart in the PERT/CPM figure would be called a Network Configuration or a *network* for short. The project software tools available today assist greatly in this area. In manually constructing the network for simple projects, and to enhance your understanding of critical path charts, you could easily end up sketching and re-sketching the network until you get it right. You would then bounce this off of others, challenge your assumptions, and make sure that you haven't left out anything vital.

TIP

Experienced network diagrammers sometimes add what is called a dummy activity wherein nothing is actually done but which helps to depict relationships between two events. Additionally, there are other charting options, all of which project management software enables you to apply to your particular model.

PLAIN ENGLISH

Dummy task   A link that shows an association or relationship between two otherwise parallel tasks along a PERT/CPM network.

ME AND MY ARROW

A highly convenient variation to the chart depicting the PERT/CPM network is called the activity-on-arrow PERT/CPM network and is depicted in the following figure.

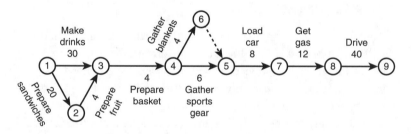

Activity-on-arrow PERT/CPM network.

Notice in this case, that the critical path line is constant, starting from Task 1, proceeding to Task 9 and noncritical activities represent diversions off the critical path. Tasks are represented by the bars with arrows. (Hence, the name "activity-on-arrow.") Events, which represent the beginning or end of a task, are depicted by numbers with a circle around them.

Gathering blankets, Task 6 leads to Event 6, which then must be connected by a dummy task, as already described. This is depicted on the chart as an arrow with a broken line leading to Event 5 (refer to the preceding figure).

Of the two possible diagrams for PERT/CPM networks, either will do. It all depends on your personal preference.

Done manually, updating a PERT/CPM network whenever there is a change in the known or estimated duration of a task can be a true pain. With software, the updating is instantaneous. If you've ever worked with spreadsheet software, you know the feeling. You plug in some new figures and, presto chango, all the monthly cash totals and the year-end cash total change immediately to reflect the latest modifications.

TIP

Once you introduce new data to your project management tools, a new critical path configuration immediately appears on your screen.

Don't Fall in Love with the Technology

Mastery of charting processes can lead to problems, particularly among technically-oriented project managers.

CAUTION

Too many project managers fall in love with technology. The tools at their disposal become intoxicating, even addictive.

Managers become overly concerned with the charts and printouts at the cost of

- Managing the project team

- Serving as a liaison to top managers and executives and stakeholders in general

- Meeting the needs of the customer or client who needs interim psychological stroking as well as ensuring that the final desired outcome will be achieved.

CAUTION

Studies of managed projects reveal that the most frequent causes of failure are nontechnical, such as the lack of commitment among project team members, hidden political agendas, and the inability of the project manager to effectively communicate project results (the subject of the next lesson).

So, use work breakdown structures, Gantt charts, and PERT/CPM networks for all their worth, but keep your eye on the people-related dynamics of the project.

The 30-Second Recap

- Managing a project of five people is far more complex than managing a project of three people. With each new person, or each new resource, far more lines of interconnectivity occur.

- For any given project, there is a critical path that the project takes and a delay in any activity along the critical path delays the overall project.

- Crashing a project means allocating additional resources to a particular task so that it is completed in less time than originally allotted. Thus, the entire project is completed in less time.

- It is easy to fall in love with the charts and technical tools available for project management today, but most project failures are a result of neglecting the human dynamic.

LESSON 9
Reporting Results

In this lesson, you learn why it is getting more difficult to report your results, how to effectively use communication tools and techniques, the importance of giving credit to your team, and the importance of assuming any blame alone.

MORE COMMUNICATIONS CHANNELS LEAD TO LESS ACCESSIBILITY

In this age of the Internet, intranets, e-mail, pagers, faxes, cell phones, and whatever else is available next, you would think that it would be easier than before to communicate your progress as you proceed on your project. Yet, it is just the opposite. The increasing number of communication vehicles have resulted in making it more difficult to get the time and attention of those to whom you must report, even when they are waiting for your report! Does this seem like a paradox?

Everyone in the working world today feels inundated by too much information at least several times during the week—if not every day and all of the time. Think back to yesteryear, when most of today's communication devices were not available. How did the typical project manager convey reports to his boss? Chances are, they worked within shouting distance of each other.

Many communication vehicles muster considerable impact for a time following their widespread acceptance in the marketplace. Twenty-five years ago, it truly was a big deal to receive a FedEx package in the morning. Now, think about how exciting it is when express packages from any vendor arrive. More often than not, they simply add to the burden of what you have already received.

Against this backdrop, is it any wonder that project managers have a more difficult time reporting results at both scheduled intervals and at random times throughout the course of their projects?

CAUTION

Even in this era when you can fax or e-mail skillfully developed WBS, Gantt, or PERT/CPM charts, there is no guarantee that your intended recipient will view them, or at least review them as scheduled.

Starting with the least technical, least involved method of communication, one person talking to another, let's proceed through widely available communication options at your disposal—with an eye on how to make them work for you to their best advantage.

IN-PERSON COMMUNICATIONS

For scheduled meetings where you have to report your progress, the key word is *preparation*. Have all your ducks in a row. Have your charts made out, your notes in order, and make bullet points of what you want to say. Chances are that the person to whom you are reporting is ultra-busy. This project may be one of many issues he or she needs to contend with.

CAUTION

If your live report is to a committee, preparation becomes even more important. Committees are more critical and less understanding than a single person. If you are using presentation software, such as Corel Presentations, PowerPoint, or any of the other popular programs, restrain yourself!

It is far too easy to go on and on, showing slide after slide in brilliant color with words that shake and sounds that go boom. This only extends the length of your presentation and takes you off the mark of what you need to be reporting.

- If you have a video to present, make it 12 minutes or less. Four minutes or less would not be too short depending on your project, how far along you are, to whom you report, and other dynamics of your organization.

TIP

Brevity is the soul of wit when it comes to making an audio-visual presentation.

- If you're using a flip chart, wall chart, white board, or other presentation hardware, prepare in advance. For flip charts and wallboards, map out and complete what you can *before* the presentation begins.

- For white boards and other media which you compose on the run, work from comprehensive notes and schematics prepared in advance so that you don't end up meandering all over the place.

Informal Person-to-Person Meetings

In informal person-to-person meetings, the same guidelines apply, except in spades. Be brief, be concise, and be gone! Don't attempt to collar anyone in the lunchroom, the hallway, the lavatory, or any other informal setting unless prior protocols for this kind of interaction have been established. You want to catch people when they are sitting down. That is when they can make notes, pick up the phone, click a mouse, staple something, whatever! When someone is standing, these types of follow-up and feedback activities aren't nearly as viable.

If you are informally asked to say a few words in a group meeting, stand and face the entire group while they are sitting. No matter what you say, this will give you a tad more authority. Again, be as concise and brief as possible. Be open to insights and take criticism. Thank the group for their attention and depart gracefully and quickly.

TELEPHONE CONTACT

Maybe your project calls for you to phone into your boss several times a day, daily, several times a week, or only every now and then. Regardless, try to schedule the actual time of the call. It is far too easy to end up with voice mail or an answering machine. This can be highly frustrating if you need an interactive conversation then and there.

If you or your boss carry a pager or cell phone and you have exchanged contact numbers with one another, hopefully you both respect each other's needs not to be unduly interrupted during the day. Such devices are excellent in situations where immediate feedback is crucial and are entirely helpful for alerting each other as to when a formal telephone meeting has been scheduled. Otherwise, they are a true pain in the neck, representing open invitations to interrupt somebody anytime or with anything.

Why is scheduling so important? Studies show that the likelihood of getting through to someone you have called at random is now less than 28 percent and falling. If you do end up talking to a machine, here are some guidelines for being as effective as you can be in that circumstance:

- Aim for a message someplace between 35 and 55 seconds. Too short, and the other party is likely to discount the importance of your message—unless, of course, it is something like, "Get out of the building! It's about to blow!"

- Longer than 55 to 60 seconds and you are likely to raise the ire of the other person who undoubtedly has been receiving messages from other people all day long.

- Speak concisely, for indeed everyone else in the world speaks hurriedly. Leave your phone number at a speed at which it actually can be written down by the respondent on the first listening. A good way to do this is to pretend that you are writing your phone number in the air with your finger as you announce it over the phone.

- Offer some gem in your message. Simply saying, "Please give me a call back," or "get back to me," is not nearly as effective as, "We need your feedback regarding what to do about the extra shipment we ordered."

E-MAIL

E-mail grows more powerful with each new version released. Popular programs such as Outlook Express, Netscape, Eudora, and Claris offer more than enough options, benefits, and features.

If you think an in-person report or phone conversation is warranted, you're probably right. Go ahead and follow through.

TIP

> If you need a "Yes" or "No" answer to a project-related question and have leeway as to when you need to get the answer, e-mail is a great tool. If you need to easily transmit report data to others waiting for it specifically via e-mail, then e-mail can also be a highly convenient reporting tool.

In general, here's a brief roster of appropriate project reporting uses of e-mail:

- Approval or disapproval

- Forwarding vital information to appropriate parties

- Data, charts, summaries, estimates, and outlines specifically requested by recipients

Sometimes e-mail can be inappropriate for reporting purposes, such as conveying

- The overly-complex

- Outlandish, highly novel, or earthshaking ideas

- Items requiring major discussion, clarification, or delicacy

- Emotionally charged information

Dr. Jaclyn Kostner says that e-mail is better than voice mail when

- A written record is needed.

- Language is a barrier. In multilanguage teams, written words are frequently easier to understand than spoken ones, especially when accents are heavy or language skills are less than fluent.

- The team's normal business day hours in each location do not match.

- You've been unable to reach the person interactively, but know the person needs the details right away.

Conversely, leave a voice mail or answering machine message when

- The sound of your voice is key to understanding your message.

- The recipient is mobile. Voice mail is easier to access than e-mail in most cases.

- Your message is urgent.

FAXES, MEMOS, AND INFORMAL NOTES

A hard-copy note in this day and age sometimes gets more attention than voice mail and e-mail. Moreover, don't underestimate the impact of a handwritten, friendly note that states something as simply as, "Making good progress on Task 2, anticipate completion by tomorrow afternoon and smooth transition to start Task 3."

If you do write by hand, be sure to use your best handwriting. It is of no value if your handwriting looks like a flea fell into an inkwell and then staggered across the page before dying.

CAUTION

> Poor penmanship has cost businesses millions of dollars due to misunderstandings, disconnections, rewrites, and revisions.

FORMALLY COMPOSED DOCUMENTS

Whether you type and print a letter to be hand delivered, sent by fax, sent by mail, or delivered by courier, be sure that you have proofread your own document. This is particularly crucial if the document is a deliverable offered in association with achieving a milestone on the project. Undoubtedly, the document will make the rounds, be copied and eventually be seen by stakeholders. Any little typo or grammatical error that you haven't corrected, even if small and not critical to your overall understanding of the document, tends to diminish your status somewhat.

As with person-to-person meetings, keep your document focused—short is better than long, concise is better than rambling. Although this varies from organization to organization and project to project, it probably makes good sense to have all of your contact information on any document that you submit to project stakeholders. This would include your name, address, phone, fax, e-mail, cell phone, pager number, car phone, and whatever other electronic leashes ensnare you.

TELECONFERENCING

Teleconferencing might take place between you, your project staff, and those to whom you are reporting, or it may simply be you alone reporting to others. They are listening on some type of speakerphone. Hence, your words need to be as clear and concise as you can practically offer.

You need to slow down your pace just a bit and make sure that words and sentences have clear endings. Even the most sophisticated speakerphones today designed for top executives and teleconferences still have major shortcomings. Not all words are clear; some words, despite the claims of manufacturers, still seem to get clipped. There is a small degree of channel noise, although this is diminishing all the time as newer and newer models appear.

Whatever you do, don't speak into a speakerphone on your end. It will sound like you are in a tin can, or at the bottom of a well. Pick up the phone and speak into the receiver or use a headset, which is widely available in office supply stores. Have your notes laid out in front of you, in sequence, so that you can offer a sequential, easy-to-understand telephone presentation.

TIP

Be prepared for the same round of observations, insights, and criticisms that you might experience in person. Teleconferencing participants are somewhat less reticent to speak up as they would be in person, but the potential is still there.

Teleconferences today often are conducted in conjunction with online presentation materials. For example, the committee hearing your report can follow your slide show in the exact sequence that you are presenting it. This can be done by uploading your presentation to the post location in advance and simply referring to each slide as numbers 1, 2, and so forth. Or, you can use a variety of Internet vendors who will assist in facilitating the transaction in real time. Check out www.MentorU.com, the leading online "faculty for hire," offering training in all manner of presentation skills. MentorU uses combination teleconferencing and online presentation technology to the utmost.

WEB-BASED PRESENTATIONS

Depending on the dynamics of your situation, you may be able to fulfill the formal aspects of your reporting requirements via Web pages. Again, the watchword here is conciseness. It is far too easy to splash lavish colors and audio and visual effects onto a Web page that really distract, rather than enhance the overall message you want to deliver.

TIP

> The page can be buried someplace within your company's Web page, part of your company's intranet placed on an independent server, or simply delivered in HTML or other hyperlink software via an e-mail attachment.

The beauty of those big computer screens that are populating people's desks these days is that the charts and slides that you send over look as magnificent on their end as they do on yours.

OH, THEM GOLDEN BULLETS

In their book, *Project Management for the 21st Century,* the authors say that "messages are golden bullets—you use them sparingly."

Too often, project managers *overcommunicate.* They spend too much time with verbiage and too little time addressing the issue at hand. Before preparing a report or delivering a presentation to any project stakeholders, consider the following:

- Will the message have strong impact, and what will be its after affects? Will someone misinterpret what you have said? Have you been as clear as you can be?

- Contemplate in advance who the receiver of your message is. This includes all receivers, those present at the time you first delivered it, and anyone else who will encounter the message later.

- To the degree that you have leverage, decide on the best medium to deliver your message and the best timing. After your organization has received bad news is not a good time to convey additional bad news.

- Stick within the boundaries that have been established. If your report is supposed to be three pages or less, keep it to three pages. If it is supposed to be delivered via fax, deliver it via fax. If it is supposed to be free of graphics, keep it free of graphics, and so on.

- Seek feedback on your message. What value is it to you if you deliver a report, and then don't get a timely response? You may head off in a slightly different direction because you didn't get the needed input in a reasonably timely manner.

INCORPORATE THE THOUGHTS OF OTHERS

Whenever you are making a report to others, either in person or via cyberspace, in real time or delayed, try to incorporate other's opinions and ideas into what you are doing. For example, you could say, "As John suggested to us the other day, we went ahead and did XYZ. This turned out quite well for all involved."

As often as possible relate within your report how you are doing. This may also dovetail with what other divisions or departments are doing and how the work may benefit the organization as a whole. Feel free to accent the milestones that you have achieved and the deliverables that you have offered, but don't go overboard.

It makes great sense to share the credit and praise for a job well done with as many people as you can. Always try to bring credit to your team even if you did the brunt of the work. Upper management tends to know what is going on regardless. The upshot is that you look like a team player and somebody who is worthy of promotion.

Conversely, accept the blame for what didn't go so well without trying to cast dispersions. You will look like a "stand up" guy or gal, and people have a secret appreciation for this.

Be entirely honest in the report when it comes to addressing your own performance. There is some leeway for tooting your own horn, but only if it is an *accurate* toot. No one likes a braggart. No one likes to read a report filled with fluff, and no one likes to be deceived. Stay on the up and up and develop your reputation as a project manager of integrity.

THE 30-SECOND RECAP

- The increasing number of communication vehicles make it more difficult to get the attention of those to whom you must report.

- For scheduled presentation of any variety the key word is *preparation*.

- A hard-copy note in this day and age sometimes gets more attention than voice mail and e-mail.

- As PC screens get larger and sharper, your reports including charts and slides that you send over look magnificent.

- Incorporate the words of others and give credit to the group, but personally accept blame. Be entirely honest when it comes to addressing your own performance.

LESSON 10
Choosing Project Management Software

In this lesson, you learn the kinds of software that are available, the capabilities of software, which software functions are crucial, and guidelines for selection.

WITH THE CLICK OF A MOUSE

Project management software today is available at a variety of prices, offering a wide variety of functions. You can use software to plan, initiate, track, and monitor your progress. You can develop reports, print individual charts, and at the push of a button (or a click of a mouse) e-mail virtually any aspect of your project plans to any team member, top manager, executive, or stakeholder.

Whereas earlier versions of PM software focused on *planning, scheduling and results*, tools for *analyzing your progress, finding critical paths*, and *asking "what if" questions* were lacking.

> **CAUTION**
> Today, there are so many options in and among so many vendors that the problem is finding your way through the bewildering choices.

Bennett Lientz and Kathryn Rea in *Project Management for the 21st Century* observe that project management software has at least five distinct differences from more widely known and used word processing, database, and spreadsheet software:

- PM software is used far less often than other categories of software.

- Fewer people use PM software, although project participants and stakeholders usually do see the generated output.

- PM software allows for more customization than many other types of software.

- PM software tends to be more expensive than commonly used, widely known types of software.

- Fewer people in your work sphere are likely to know how to use PM software.

LEAVE A GOOD THING ALONE

Project management software went from being expensive and crude, to less expensive and highly functional, to even less expensive, but confusing. When Harvard Project Manager was launched in 1983 it represented a breakthrough in PM software. Its main focus was on project budgeting, scheduling, and resource management. With Harvard Project Manager you were able to generate Gantt charts, PERT/CPM charts, and a variety of other charts and tables. It was considered an integrated project planning and control package and sold for as little as 30 percent of the price of its clunky, less functional predecessors.

In the two decades that followed, competition among PM software vendors heated up, prices came down, and functionality went sky high. Many packages now are harder to learn and use. Consider your own experience in using word processing, database, or spreadsheet software. Aren't there earlier versions of current programs that were easier and more convenient? You were able to pop them in, learn them in a day or so, and go on your merry way.

Today, with expanding megabyte counts, it seems that the vendors need to have everything plus the kitchen sink. This gives them the opportunity to design splashy ads listing umpteen features. Real-istically, how many people are true power users who would use all of the advertised features?

CAUTION

> Whereas the Harvard Project Manager could be learned in as little as a day if you were diligent, cur-rent PM software can take as much as five days of your time, if you are starting from square one and have no PC guru or mentor nearby to steer you along.

Whose Choice Is It?

Certainly, if your organization, department or division already uses or prefers a certain type of software, then your decision is already made. Your quest becomes mastering that software—or at least the parts of it that are crucial for you to know.

TIP

> If a brand of PM software is the preferred choice in your workplace, and other projects employ such soft-ware, you are relatively fortunate. Other project managers or staff will know how to use it and can serve as *ad-hoc* software gurus to you.

With no experienced users in your work setting, some important ques-tions arise:

- **What kind of software should be chosen?**   In choosing PM software a rule of thumb is to choose a popular and very well-known package. The price is likely to be highly compet-itive, people around you would have either heard of the ven-dor or have heard that the software is widely known, and you won't have to spend a lot of time defending your decision!

- **Who should learn it?**   If you and you alone will have responsibility for learning the software, you need to build time and expense into your budget—it will take you time to learn it or to take a course, and your time has a cost.

TIP

The Project Management Institute at www.pmi.org and the Project Management Control Tower at www.4pm.com each offer a wide variety of books, audio-visual materials, training guides, classroom training, seminars, and increasingly, online training. Also, PMFORUM at www.ProjectManager.com offers a host of career opportunities for project managers or those seeking to enter the profession.

While it may seem obvious that you as the project manager should be the primary user of PM software, you may need to rethink that assumption. Depending on what you are managing and the dynamics of your organization, if you were to be the primary software user, you might spend the brunt of your time working with the software and have precious little time left for forming and building your team, maintaining reporting requirements, and offering the overall kind of day-to-day project management that the venture requires.

Recognizing the danger of having a project manager become too immersed with project management software, some organizations have established support groups or provide internal software gurus. These gurus are the in-house experts and are often loaned to project management teams for the duration of the project.

The gurus work directly with the project manager, incorporating his feedback, answering his questions, and undertaking whatever types of analysis the project manager requests. They routinely maintain schedules, budget reports, and track the allocation of resources. An experienced software guru knows how and how often to share project related reports with project staff and project stakeholders in general.

WHAT'S YOUR PLEASURE?

Assuming that you're not in the position where your organization will loan someone to you who will handle the brunt of PM software activities and assuming that there is no particular program of choice yet established, how do you go about selecting software?

First, establish what kind of user you're going to be, which is largely determined by two elements: the size of your project and how technical you are.

For tiny projects of zero to two staff for a project of a few months or less, it's possible that no project management software is necessary! How so? You may already possess all the software and software knowledge you need to be effective in managing a small project. We're talking about spreadsheets, word processing, a graphics or drawing program, and the functionality to generate tables, graphs, flow charts, and other diagrams.

TIP

Though somewhat makeshift, the combination of reports and exhibits that you can muster with your current software and skills might be more than adequate for your project needs.

Your current software may be entirely adequate if the basic work breakdown structure (WBS) and a Gantt chart or two is all you need, and you don't necessarily have to create a critical path.

For projects involving four or more people, extending several months or longer, with a variety of critical resources, it makes sense to invest in some type of software. Again, it doesn't necessarily need to be PM software per se. Many calendar and scheduling software programs come with built-in functions. You can produce tables, Gantt charts, and even maintain a schedule for four to ten people. Increasingly, you can do this on hand-held computers.

> **TIP**
>
> With a total project management team of four people, extended over several months, employing dedicated PM software may make the most sense.

Dedicated PM Software

The competition among dedicated PM software vendors is keen. Major vendors in the field include PlanView, Inc., Primavera, Microsoft, Dekker Welcome, and Artemus. (An overview of PM software with descriptions can be found in the next lesson.) There are also lower-end programs that will help you generate plans, project reports, and basic charts that don't require as much learning time. Products such as Quick Gantt, Milestone Simplicity, and Project Vision sell for less than $100 and are available at office superstores as well as retail software stores.

> **TIP**
>
> Inexpensive PM software may be your best option if you don't have anyone else in the organization who can serve as guru, but you do wish to automate, rather than manually generate critical reports and charts.

Suppose that you are managing many people over many months, and have a thousand or more tasks and subtasks to complete. Here, you would look at PM software for midrange project managers. You can spend anywhere from $200 to $6,000 using the more feature-laden versions of software named above. Most packages will give you the full range of tools sought by even veteran project managers on multiyear projects.

The problem with software at this level is that you can quickly become a slave to it. For example, will you decide to schedule and track all subtasks and tasks based on identified start times, stop times, for each staff member, all the time? Or, will you continually rely on your staff to give you estimates of tasks and subtask completion times?

- Relying on the input of your staff helps to build a team, but it takes more work.

- Using the software is arduous at first, saves time later, and keeps your head in front of a PC screen more often—away from the people and the events happening all around you.

High-end project management software is designed for the very largest, longest duration, most involved types of projects. If you are a high-end user, you wouldn't have picked up this book. Here, we are talking about software that can range from a few thousand to several thousand dollars. Learning such packages could take weeks. The software selection process alone could take weeks or months.

CAUTION

> Even if at the high end there are so many programs available, made by such vendors as Cobra, Semantic, Instaplan, Klavis (for Mac users), Open Plan, Primavera, Microsoft, Enterprise PM, Microplanner, and others, that you would need a consultant to make such a selection.

Regardless of your level of PM software knowledge, your selection could be one of the most important factors in overall project success. Many project managers have found that the software in force is too complex and too unwieldy to use for the entire project. Some end up using only an element of the software, such as budgeting or scheduling; some use it only for making charts; others end up abandoning the software midstream. Undoubtedly, a whole lot of scrambling follows because whatever the software was used for now needs to be done manually.

How Will You Use PM Software?

The first time, modest users obviously won't use PM software the way that an experienced pro will. Nevertheless, there are levels of usage worth differentiating:

- **Reporting**   Here the project manager uses the software to generate Gantt or, possibly, PERT/CPM charts. She may use other software programs such as word processing and spreadsheets to supplement her project graphs and produce reports.

- **Tracking**   The software is used to compare actual versus planned progress. As the project staff completes tasks and subtasks, the results of their efforts are logged so that the tracking effort stays current.

PLAIN ENGLISH

Project tracking   A system for identifying and documenting progress performance for effective review and dissemination to others.

- **What-if**   The PM software is engaged to identify the impact of shuffling resources, changing the order of subtasks, or changing tasks' dependencies. What-if analysis is kind of fun, because you get immediate feedback.

CAUTION

Change one variable at a time to have a full grasp of its impact. If you change too many variables at once, the picture becomes cloudy.

- **Cost control**   Project managers use PM software to allocate costs to various project resources. This is usually done by figuring out how much resource time and effort is consumed. Lientz and Rea observe that "most project management software systems lack flexibility in handling costs as well as interfaces into budgeting and accounting systems." Thus, the cost computations that a project manager makes generally don't plug into the overall cost structures the accountants in her organization work with.

- **Clocking**   By adding project team member hours expended on various tasks and subtasks on a regular basis, project managers can then generate reports showing actual versus scheduled use of resources.

CHECKLISTS AND CHOICES

It's hard to generalize what type of software various levels of users may require, but here are some general criteria worth considering:

- **Ease of use**   Is the software easy to plug in, are there good help screens, is there a tutorial, is there strong customer support, and is the software menu driven and intuitive? Is it easy to move things around, are the commands as standard as possible and easy to learn? Is there an accompanying manual that is easy to read? Are you able to get started on some functions quickly?

- **Reporting functions**   Does the program allow for individual revising of report formats, can these be easily imported into other software programs, and can they easily be saved, added to, combined, and read?

- **Charting capacity**   Does the software offer the basic project management charts (virtually all do), is there automatic recalculation, are there easy-to-use options, and are there drag and drop capabilities? Can charts be imported and exported easily, are supporting graphics easy to see and to use, and can charts readily be changed into other forms?

- **Calendar generators**   Does this software allow for calendars of all durations, in a variety of formats, for different aspects of the project and project staff, with the ability to mark particular days and times, with holidays and other nonworking days pre-programmed, and are these calendars also easily importable and exportable?

- **Interfacing**   Can you easily connect with telecommunication systems and is information easily shared with others who require online access? Is it efficient in terms of byte space consumed?

- **Report generation**   Can a variety of report formats be selected, with quick changing capabilities, and easy transference to word processing software?

In addition, consider these attributes:

- Shows onscreen previews of reports prior to printing

- Offers a variety of formats for Gantt and PERT charts

- Works with a variety of printers and other equipment

- Enables several projects to share a common pool of resources

- Conveys cost data by task or by time

- Allows printing of subsections of charts

- Accepts both manual and automatic schedule updates

Most of the vendors you will encounter have such capabilities. Hence, you need to go beyond a strict comparison of software functionality and consider the attributes, benefits, and services of using a particular vendor as well. In fact, for any major purchase it's advisable to have a good set of questions. The following is a list adapted from my book *The Complete Idiot's Guide to Managing Stress*. Ask the vendors whether they

- Offer any corporate, government, association, military, and educators' discounts?

- Have weekly, monthly, or quarterly seasonal discounts?
- Offer off-peak discounts?
- Guarantee the lowest price?
- Accept major credit cards?
- Accept orders by fax or e-mail?
- Have a money-back guarantee, or other guarantee?
- Use a 1-800 ordering fax line?
- Guarantee shipping dates?
- Have a toll-free customer service line?
- Avoid selling, renting, or otherwise using your name and ordering information?
- Insure shipments?
- Charge for shipping and handling?
- Include tax?
- Have any other charges?
- Have demos?
- Offer free or low-cost upgrades?
- Have references available?
- Keep a list of satisfied customers in your area?
- Have been in business long?
- Have standard delivery times?
- Warranty the product?

Making a List, Checking It Twice

After you've established your own set of selection criteria in consideration of all the things that your project entails and in consideration of the various attributes, benefits and features of working with each vendor, engage in a useful exercise: Decide on paper what you *must have* versus what it is *nice to have* versus what is *not needed,* but you will take it if it is offered.

Then, using articles, product reviews, and the vendors' Web sites, make a preliminary survey of the various packages available and how they stack up. A simple matrix or grid with the vendors listed across the top representing columns, and the important attributes to you down the left side of the page will suffice.

CAUTION

Selection processes can be brutal. You may encounter ten or twelve possible vendors, but try to knock down the list early to three to five. Sometimes, a particular feature is so outstanding that it outweighs other mediocre elements of a vendor's overall package.

Most vendors will readily offer you product demonstrations. Down loadable product demos often are available at the vendor's Web site. Otherwise, demos can often be observed over the Internet.

TIP

Some vendors allow you to download a full package, available for a limited duration.

If you've narrowed the field to three or four vendors, you have a fighting chance of identifying the one that best meets your needs.

TIP

> If at all possible, observe the software *actually in use* either in your own organization or someplace else.

Observing software in use is most telling. Someone in the field, actually using the software, can provide first-person input as to where the software shines and doesn't shine. You get far richer information than you can get from a Web site or, for that matter, a product demo.

THE 30-SECOND RECAP

- PM software has become more sophisticated and more bewildering. Many packages will do the jobs you need to do, but are so difficult to learn and to master that you waste valuable resources, namely your time. Worse, you end up abandoning the package.

- Many organizations loan software gurus to a project or have other project managers who can supply ad hoc mentoring. If this applies to you, consider yourself fortunate.

- Don't get so immersed in software that you lose contact with your project team and the environment that surrounds you.

- Choosing the right software may be vital. Predetermine your selection criteria so that you're not buffeted by an endless array of options, benefits and features.

LESSON 11
A Sampling of Popular Programs

In this lesson, you learn which software programs are popular, what vendors have to say about their own programs, and how to get in touch with vendors.

YESTERDAY'S NEWS

As each day passes, any software program evaluation presented in any book ages and soon becomes obsolete. Consequently, the surveys and review of products listed in this lesson are presented for the sake of example only!

A survey titled "Tools of the Trade: A Survey of Project Management Tools" appeared in the September 1998 issue of the *Project Management Journal.* The *Journal* evaluated what the authors called "Top Project Management Tools." Some 159 project managers responded to survey questions out of 1,000 managers initially contacted. The typical respondent had slightly more than 10 years of project management experience and slightly more than 12 years' experience in the field of information systems. Hence, this was a select group of veteran project managers.

The 159 respondents cited 79 different project management tools that they either were using currently or had used within three years. Of note, the top 10 of these 79 tools were identified by three-quarters of the respondents. The top 10 tools in order were

1. Microsoft Project

2. Primavera Project Planner

3. Microsoft Excel

4. Project Workbench

5. Time Line

6. Primavera SureTrak

7. CA-SuperProject

8. Project Scheduler

9. Artemis Prestige

10. FasTracs

Microsoft Project was the most frequently used PM software at the time of the survey. This is somewhat understandable. In the late 1990s, Microsoft dominated all channels of software advertising and promotion.

Artemis Prestige, Primavera Project Planner, and Project Scheduler were sited as being used more often for projects lasting six months or longer. However, for overall satisfaction with project management software, the ratings were close, with Project Scheduler first, followed by Primavera Project Planner, Project Workbench, Microsoft Excel, Primavera SureTrak, and CA-SuperProject. Thereafter, the score began to fall off a bit.

These programs were rated as to content, accuracy, format, ease of use, timeliness, and then given an overall rating. The top five or six choices in terms of overall satisfaction closely matched the top five or six software packages for which project managers routinely received the most training within their organizations.

However, FasTracs was one product for which managers routinely had no hours of training, and yet it received a remarkably high score. This was especially true in terms or "overall adequacy" when respondents were asked how many months they had been working with the various software products, and how many hours a week they spent using them.

Thus, based on this one study, FasTracs would be the product of choice for the first-time or light user, if all things could be held constant.

TIP

Not surprisingly, the training time that project managers received for the various software packages (that they were charged with learning) influenced how adequate they thought the software to be. Said alternatively, the more training you have to work with a particular type of project management software, the higher you tend to rate that software.

Armed and Online

Flash forward to today, when more and more project management tools have an online component. The power and capability of such programs is awesome.

The following is but a snapshot in time as to what is available now, largely in the words of the vendors themselves.

CAUTION

The array of software options available today is even more bewildering than that of years ago.

PlanView

PlanView provides all-browser software within a Windows environment for managers, employees, and others throughout the enterprise—as well as partners, vendors, and service providers in the extended enterprise. The software helps manage projects and other work, update employee information, and manage the workforce. PlanView optimizes the staffing of multiple projects by taking into account the skills and true availability of your workforce. Thus, PlanView enables an enterprise to measure all work and to manage to its full capacity.

PlanView is delivered by user role. That could be managers, employees, and others throughout the enterprise—as well as partners, vendors, and service providers. PlanView Online is an integrated project and workforce management system, is 100 percent Web software, and features

- Personalized Web portal

- Self-administration by staff

- Collaborative critical path engine

- Support for your project office

- Viewing workforce capacity

- Integrated time and expense tracking

- Project delivery model

PlanView uses an enterprise Web portal to manage workplace access to information and applications. The enterprise portal is the workers' interface to the PlanView intranet or extranet. The features available to each role are tailored for each customer.

Managers, employees, and business partners sign on to PlanView through a dynamically built Web page called HomeView. Each person's HomeView portal reflects his rights to the information in the central repository and the unique needs of his role in the enterprise.

When the user signs on to the system, his or her profile is recalled, and a unique set of features is placed on the menu for his or her use. PlanView calls these FeatureSets, and they provide access to the rest of the functions of the PlanView suite. For instance, a project manager has access to her project portfolio, the scheduling engines, and approval of status information. A contributor will report time, expenses, and remaining work and update his skills.

Users' favorite Web links for discussion groups, project or department Web sites, as well as executables for key software like a virtual meeting software, project sites, and methodology content providers are all easily accessed.

TIP

> Reminders let users track events with knowledge of current time, to inform them when events are due.

DEKKER

Dekker TRAKKER project management software offers many enhanced features, such as enhanced integration with Oracle and SQL Server for complete enterprise control and enhanced human interface to simplify data entry through spreadsheet views. The software also does the following:

- Provides the ability to utilize Microsoft Access for Workgroup and offline data requirements.

- Increases system performance.

- Provides user-defined three-dimensional bar charts.

- Provides configurable milestone and bar colors.

- Enables enhanced curve loading.

- Yields real-time calculation.

- Offers ABC and Gantt view screens.

The Gantt view screen, for example, offers selectable three-dimensional activity bars, user-defined bar style, customizable colors, configurable columns, integrated baseline control, interim milestones on a single line, user-defined milestone symbols, fiscal and standard time scale, and real-time calculation.

The ABC View Screen offers selectable data row, values in heads, quantity dollars, burdens, configurable columns, the new Trakker spreadsheet view for familiar data entry, integrated baseline control, real-time calculation, and complete cost and schedule integration.

PRIMAVERA

Primavera SureTrak Project Manager recognizes a project team's need for constant, timely project communications and updates. Primavera bolstered its SureTrak with Web publishing enhancements that let users quickly and easily save project layouts and reports in HTML format. The Web Publishing Wizard can then group and sort the tabular and graphical HTML reports and layouts from all your projects, into a single, easy-to-read project Web site that can be conveniently viewed by the whole team.

Based on extensive usability testing, SureTrak simplifies project management for mainstream use by addressing the ease-of-use needs of novice project managers, while delivering project management applications for small-to-medium–sized projects. Its rich feature offering includes advanced organization of project plans, activities, and team members; Project KickStart for step-by-step project plan creation; Progress Spotlight for easy updating of project activities and Web Publishing Wizard for enhanced online communications among team members.

The Variable Timescale feature lets users zoom in on a portion of the project time scale. For example, activities scheduled for the next month can be displayed in days, while the rest of the project is displayed in weeks or months. This feature presents the details for one period of interest, while still displaying the entire project on one page.

To give project teams greater insight into the sequence of interrelated project tasks, SureTrak 3.0 includes an intuitive PERT Timescale display.

SureTrak builds on existing customization capabilities, by enabling users to modify an individual or group of bars based on activity attributes. By combining new display options with colors and patterns, project managers will be able to graphically communicate valuable project details and status for analysis.

SureTrak includes several other new capabilities, designed specifically to simplify use of the software. In addition to an updated user interface that adheres to accepted 32-bit operating environments, users will find they are more productive when analyzing alternative what-if scenarios for their projects, by taking advantage of new options for using project filters and display layouts.

OTHER PRIMAVERA PRODUCTS

With P3e you can manage the entire project lifecycle. P3e is a total project management solution, encompassing all aspects of the project lifecycle. It combines all of the in-depth project management capabilities required by project-driven managers.

Through costs, schedule, and earned value thresholds, or variances, P3e automatically generates issues when thresholds are exceeded by project elements. Project managers can prioritize resulting issues and let P3e send e-mail alerts to the responsible parties to ensure prompt resolution. To make sure that project risks are properly identified and quantified, P3e also integrates risk management and assesses the impact of those risks. P3e quickly performs what-if simulation to determine the schedule and cost exposure of project risks based on estimated impacts and probability factors.

TIP

Risks can be categorized and risk control plans can be documented as part of the overall project plan.

Prima Progress Reporter provides full workgroup support and coordination of project resources with minimum training and hassle. Each team member receives activity assignments—even across multiple projects. Team members use Progress Reporter to communicate timesheet and activity status to the project manager and project database via the LAN, remotely via e-mail, and over the Internet.

Primavera Portfolio Analyst provides unparalleled project summary and tracking information to executives, senior managers, and project analysts through a rich set of graphics, spreadsheets, and reports. The Project Portfolio wizard groups together any number of projects, based on project attributes or hierarchy, for comparison and analysis. Portfolio Analyst's interactive interface allows quick drill-down to see information at any level of detail for clear presentation and discussion.

P3e combined with Portfolio Analyst and Progress Reporter form the most advanced solution for managing all projects within an enterprise.

WELCOM

Welcom offers "Project Management for a Changing World." Welcom is a global distribution of project management software, providing leading tools to corporations worldwide. The Welcom product line includes totally integrated and versatile software for managing both in-house and enterprise-wide projects.

Welcom has joined Pacific Edge Software to define the XML (Extensible Markup Language) schema for project management.

TIP

The flexible business-to-business schema will enable intelligent project data exchange between an organization's information systems.

MICROSOFT

The best way to manage your projects is to have the information you need right in front of you. Microsoft Project 2000 gives you that information by providing flexible tools for organizing, viewing and analyzing project data and by allowing your team members to update their status through the Web—another way of making The Business Internet work for you.

Since the most accurate status information comes from those doing the work, Microsoft Project 2000 includes a simple, Windows-based interface that team members can access from their Web browsers to provide collaborative input. It's called Microsoft Project Central, and it can give you up-to-the-minute data that will help you to make the best decisions for your business.

PROJECT KICKSTART

Project KickStart is a powerful, but easy-to-use planning tool that helps you design, organize, and schedule *any* project. Project Kick-Start's eight-step planning process focuses your attention on the structure of the project, the goals, resources, risks, and strategic issues critical to your project's success. Your plan is ready in 30 minutes.

Schedule your project using the pop-up calendar and Gantt chart. Print out a to-do list or one of the seven presentation-ready reports. Or, for added versatility "hot link" your plan into Microsoft Project, SureTrak, P3, FastTrack Schedule, Super Project, Project Scheduler 7, Time Line, Milestones Etc., WBS Chart, Word, WordPerfect, and Excel.

Some of the features and benefits include

- The ability to work with any size project up to 750 tasks and 75 resources.

- Sample projects packed with information, and ready to use.

- Drag-and-drop hints from libraries of goals, phases, and obstacles.

- Gantt chart for "big picture" scheduling.

- Seven presentation-ready reports.

- Saving as HTML—post project plans on your Intranet.

- Hot-link to Word, WordPerfect and Excel—include project plans in proposals and business plans.

- Hot-link to other PM software.

- Free technical support.

Project KickStart requires no project management training to use and comes with a helpful (and knowledgeable) "advisor" and free, friendly telephone support.

TIP

By working through the program's icons and organizing your project step by step, you'll develop a clear overview of the project and what it will take to complete it. You become totally in control—more efficient, more effective, more successful.

The next time your boss asks for a project plan or your staff demands a marketing strategy, just click on Project KickStart. This breakthrough program will help you design, organize, and schedule your project in only 30 minutes.

- It's fast and easy—no training required. Your plan is ready in minutes!

- Plan with complete confidence. With Project KickStart, nothing is overlooked. Nothing is forgotten.

- Schedule the way you want. It is your choice. Use Project KickStart's built-in Gantt chart for small to mid-size projects. Or hot-link data to Microsoft Project and other software for added functionality.

THE 30-SECOND RECAP

- PM software changes so rapidly that no book is published fast enough to review the latest software.

- The more training a project manager has with a particular type of PM software, the more highly he or she tends to rate that software. Hence, training is important!

- Many vendors now offer total online project management capabilities.

- Many vendors offer software support, and with the complexity of the programs they sell, support is crucial.

LESSON 12

Multiple Bosses, Multiple Projects, Multiple Headaches

In this lesson, you learn how to keep your wits on multiple projects, help your bosses not to overload you, handle multiple reporting structures, and be assertive when overload seems unavoidable.

PARTICIPATING ON MORE THAN ONE PROJECT AT A TIME

Sometimes you're asked to manage this and asked to manage that. Managing more than one project at a time is more difficult than managing a single project, but it is not impossible. People do it all the time, and with a few observations and insights, you can get good at it as well.

Sometimes organizations assign smaller projects to up-and-coming managers, such as you, as a form of on-the-job training. By letting you get your feet wet on small fleeting projects, you are better prepared to tackle larger ones. Some companies also assign newly hired staff to serve as project team members on small projects so that they will have a wider view of company operations and, in time, manage some of the smaller projects themselves on their path to leading larger projects.

As you will see in Lesson 14, "Learning from Your Experience," all the skills that you acquire and all the insights and experience you gain represent grist for the mill.

> **TIP**
>
> When managed properly, small projects (even one-person projects) still contain some of the essential elements found in the largest of projects.

By its nature, project management is a short-term, challenging endeavor. The opportunity to tackle small projects and even a series of small projects simultaneously is a worthwhile career challenge.

As you hone your planning, monitoring, and overall organizational skills, you become a far more valuable employee to your organization. After all, they have had other projects in the past in which managers failed to achieve the desired outcome, budgets were overrun, time frames were missed by a mile, morale dropped to zero, and chaos ruled.

> **TIP**
>
> Reframe your focus about participating in or even managing multiple projects as opportunities worth mastering.

COMPLEXITY HAPPENS

Suppose you're not formally assigned the task of managing two projects at once or having two projects overlap in terms of time interval. Chances are that you still face general issues related to managing multiple priorities. If so, you are not alone. An increasing number of career professionals seem to be affected by this same phenomenon.

Why is it that things seem to be getting more complex? The increase in both size and usage of the Internet means that information is disseminated at much greater speeds and volumes than at any time before. Information is power, as you've rapidly learned, and people use it to market or sell goods, construct new organizations, or create new ways to get a jump on the competitor.

In addition, the increasing use of technology in our society ensures that you will have more to contend with. In North America today, we face a major technological breakthrough every 17 minutes. This is as much as 3 or 4 an hour, 70 to 80 a day, and thousands per year. We will soon be in an environment where there are 17 technological breakthroughs every minute, with hundreds of associated services.

Perhaps most onerous for the project manager, as we proceed into the future and society becomes more complex, more stringent documentation is often required by the government, customers, and others. No project goes unscathed. It's unfortunate, but it seems it's getting harder and harder to do anything without documentation. Hiring or firing someone, buying a product, selling something, expanding, merging, casting off—almost any business function you can name requires more documentation, which contributes to each of us having to handle an increasing amount of work.

A Diffuse Pattern

In many organizations, you may encounter scores and scores of small-to-medium–sized projects with various starting and stopping times throughout the year. Often, some of these projects are not large enough or complicated enough to require the services of a full-time project manager. In such cases, somebody may be asked to manage a project while still maintaining much of the responsibility for their principle role in some other department or elsewhere in the organization.

Such project managers may also find themselves in charge of several small projects whose time-frames overlap by varying degrees. If you're put in charge of a variety of small projects, you need to mentally separate them and to stay focused on each.

A Tale of Two Offices

My friend and fellow speaker, Al Walker from Columbia, South Carolina, managed two projects a few years ago with aplomb. As a professional speaker, Al had the continuing task of preparing for his roster of scheduled speeches coming up. In such cases, he had to ensure that flights were made, project materials delivered to the meeting planner in plenty of time, all hotel accommodations were made and so on. On top of that, he was elected to the presidency of the National Speakers Association, a post that lasted one fiscal year.

TIP

> Managing multiple projects may be less of a burden than you anticipate. After all, in your own career, whether you can call them projects or not, you probably have already perfected techniques for handling a variety of simultaneous issues or priority items.

Al took on the responsibility admirably. He knew that more than 3200 members of the organization were counting on him for effective leadership. To establish a separate focus, Al rearranged his corporate offices so that he had a distinct and separate office for his speaking business and for his role as NSA president.

As he walked from one office to another, his focus and attention shifted dramatically in seconds. He even had different phone lines installed and duplicate supporting equipment so that he did not have to shuttle items back and forth between the offices.

TIP

> The key to managing multiple projects is to maintain a clear and separate focus so that when you are working on Project 1, Project 1 is the only thing in your mind, and likewise when you are working on Project 2.

Extravagance is Not Necessary

Al's approach may sound extravagant. After all, you have to have both the space to set up an additional office and the resources to stock both offices adequately for the projects at hand. Yet, most people can do something nearly the same. Who doesn't have doubles on certain types of office equipment? Nearly everyone has the room to carve out additional space, perhaps not in a physically distinct office or cubicle. Yet, somewhere else with your office, or organization, home, vacation home, or other physical space you have.

Start up procedures and the associated burdens for creating a second office or work area are more than offset by the mental clarity and emotional resilience you engender. Once you're able to maintain the two work areas, managing two projects becomes more viable.

CAUTION

Does this mean that if you are managing three projects it would be advisable to create a third office? Not necessarily. You can carry this concept too far.

When faced with two major projects of fairly equal weight and complexity the "two office spaces" approach works as well as any.

Reporting to More Than One Boss at a Time

Related to the issue of managing multiple projects is having to deal with multiple bosses—either on one project or on several projects. The immediate recognizable challenge is that either boss is likely to encroach on the schedule you have already devised in pursuit of the assignments doled out by the other boss.

Understandably, you may experience a range of anxieties and concerns when having to relay to one boss that plans may have to be delayed because of other activities you are involved with. Relations with all bosses in the case of a multiple boss situation need to be handled delicately. After all, depending on your organization, bosses may

- Have the power to fire you on a moment's notice without consulting anyone else.

- Conduct performance appraisals of you that dramatically impact your ability to advance in the company.

- Define your job responsibilities. Indeed, they personally may have written your job description.

- Schedule your work activities. In this respect, your boss may have control over each and every hour that you spend at work, what you work on, how quickly you have to work, and what resources you're provided.

- Have leverage over what benefits you receive.

You may find yourself having to become professionally assertive with your various bosses. Stay open and candid with them so that you *don't end up promising everything to everybody and thereby creating incredible pressure on yourself!* Here are some suggestions for dealing with each of your multiple bosses:

- Praise your bosses when they merit praise. Many employees forget that the boss is a person, too, and one who needs psychological strokes just like everyone else.

- Assemble your evidence. If you have a point to make, come in armed with supporting artifacts.

- Don't dump on your boss. Your boss is not a shoulder to cry on for what went wrong at home or on the project.

- Pace your communications. Don't overwhelm your boss with more than he or she can comfortably ingest. Your project may be only one of many.

- Take personal responsibility for any departmentwide activities or projects in which you're participating.

- Don't drone on. Present your situation or problem as succinctly as you can, while maintaining an effective level of interpersonal communication.

WORKAHOLIC FOR HIRE

What about the situation where you are flat out asked to do too much, take on too much work, stay too many hours or handle more than you're comfortable handling? In such cases, the ability to assert yourself becomes a valuable one. Suppose you work for a boss who's a borderline workaholic. No, make that a full-fledged workaholic. How do you keep your job, turn in a good performance, maintain sufficient relations, and still have a life? As I pointed out in *The Complete Idiot's Guide Assertiveness*, you say *no* without making it sound like *no*:

- "That is something I'd really like to tackle, but I don't think it would be in our best interest since I'm already on XYZ."

- "I can certainly get started on it, but because of the DEF deadline and the XYZ event, I'm certain I won't be able to get into it full swing until the middle of next month."

- "If we can park that one for a while, I'm sure I can do a good job on it. As you know, I'm already handling the HIJ and wouldn't want to proceed unless I could do a bang-up job. If you're eager to have somebody get started on this right away, I wouldn't hesitate to suggest Tom."

- "Hmmm, help me here; I'm not sure what level priority this should be in light of the lineup I'm already facing ...."

DON'T WIMP OUT ON YOURSELF

Too many professionals today, fearful that they may lose their job as well as their health and other benefits, suffer various forms of work-related abuse because they lack the ability to assert themselves.

The following is some additional language, mildly more forceful, that you may need to draw upon depending on circumstances:

- "I'm stretched out right now on Project A to the full extent of my resources, and if I take this on, not only will I not be able to give it my best effort, but the other things I'm handling will suffer as well."

- "I'm going to request that I not be put on Project D, if that's okay with you. I've been going long and hard for several months now, and if I don't regain some sense of personal balance I feel I'm putting health at risk."

- "Is there anyone else right now who could take on that project? I need to get a better handle on what I'm already managing."

- "I wish I could—I've been burning the candle at both ends on Project A, and if I start to burn it in the middle, there will be nothing left."

ASSERTING YOURSELF IN DIRE SITUATIONS

Suppose despite your protestations to the contrary, your boss or bosses keep piling on the work and responsibilities. No matter how effective you are at asserting yourself and how often you do it, you seem to be besieged with more assignments and more projects. Here are the basic options:

- You can push for a compromise situation where you take on *some* of the new work. Or, you can take all of it on, but you'll have to receive additional project resources, such as more people, bigger budget, or more equipment.

- You can knuckle under and simply take on the added assignments with no additional resources. (Avoid this!)

Instead, compute how many staff hours will be necessary to tackle the added assignment, how much that would cost, and what the overall return would be. Likewise, if you need a bigger budget in general, new equipment, or other project resources, figure it out and ask for it!

THE 30-SECOND RECAP

- Constant advances in technology make us constant multi-taskers. This is a valuable and marketable skill. Managing more than one project at a time is achievable if you can successfully separate your responsibilities—mentally and maybe even physically.

- Remember that your bosses are human, too—and at least as busy as you are. Respect their time by being concise and organized in your communications, but don't hesitate to issue kudos and praise when they are due.

- Sometimes, you have to assert your own rights, as a person with a life, and you have to be assertive in declining additional responsibilities or requesting more support.

- When you still are asked to take on more than you can comfortably handle, don't hesitate to ask for a compromise, or additional resources, or both.

Lesson 13

A Construction Mini-Case

In this lesson, you learn how a thorough initial research phase can pay off handsomely for your project, that open and easy communication is critical to your project's success, the difference between getting by and excelling, and that simple solutions often are best.

HELPING CONSTRUCTION SITE MANAGERS TO BE MORE EFFECTIVE

Bob works for a large metropolitan construction firm that handles anywhere from 20 to 40 projects in a given year ranging from new home construction, office buildings, and parking lots, to assorted public works projects. Each project is headed by a project foreman who has various assistants and has anywhere from 5 to 25 crew members who perform the heavy labor.

Much like any company in the construction field, the company has had its ups and downs over the past several years. Regional weather patterns, shrinking municipal budgets, new competition in the market place, and a host of other factors keep upper management on their toes.

One of the biggest bug-a-boos in the business, as noted by the owner, is due to declining profitability per job even as the company matures. It was the owner's belief that as a cadre of highly experienced, well-trained foremen were established, the profit potential on jobs should improve somewhat.

Yet, things didn't seem to be working. Even on construction jobs that represented fourth or fifth jobs for a regular client, where all parties involved were relatively old hands at various processes, profits were down.

A thorough audit of the company's practices revealed that the critical issue was high turnover among labor crews. All other factors, such as slight increases in cost of materials, increases in wages, licenses, permits, bonding, insurance, and the dozens of other issues that go hand in hand with initiating new constructions were handled relatively well. In fact, compared to other comparably sized companies in the field, this particular company was above average in many categories.

LET'S ASSIGN IT TO A PROJECT MANAGER

Bob was put in charge of a project authorized directly by the owner to determine why the company was experiencing higher than normal turnover rates among its construction crews, and then, most importantly, to develop a strategy that would lower turnover rates to that of the industry and regional standards.

Using the very same software that the company employed to manage individual construction projects, Bob initiated a project of his own, called "Overturning Turnover," or "OT" for short. Bob was the solo staff person on the project, no one reported to him; all responsibilities were up to him. On top of that, the owner had precious little time to spend with Bob, as he was often up to the state capitol to lobby on certain issues and was the chief marketer for the company as well as the chief purchasing officer.

So, Bob laid out a plan on his own, based on his experience in the industry. He knew that he would need to talk to each of the foremen to get their views, several of their assistants, and the onsite crew chief and vocal leaders.

TIP

> Bob chose to eyeball each of the construction sites and talk to all the players involved face to face, as opposed to using the telephone, even though many of the foremen would have opened up to him over the phone.

Bob felt certain that the key to successfully completing this project and devising a strategy that would overturn turnover would be found largely at the sites themselves. In the days that followed, Bob made the rounds, carved out some time with all of the participants he thought to be important to speak to, and carefully logged in his notes.

ARM CHAIR ANALYSIS VERSUS ONSITE OBSERVATION

After just his third visit to a construction site, Bob had what he thought was a breakthrough, but wanted to confirm his findings and continued to maintain his visitation schedule. Bob's major observation was that the project foremen were largely white, Anglo-Saxon, English-speaking males (this was no surprise to Bob), whereas over the years, there were increasing numbers of foreign-born workers who comprised the construction crews.

The company's far-flung empire stretched out over several counties and included projects in major urban and suburban areas from which the company recruited its labor. In past years, there had been many Spanish-speaking laborers, many of whom knew sufficient English to get by. Moreover, among any crew with five or more Spanish-speaking laborers, at least one of them spoke fluent English. So, the language barrier did not seem to be a problem among Hispanics, even between the foreman and a non-English–speaking worker, because there was always a liaison person nearby.

As the entire region began to be inhabited by a more diverse population, construction crews themselves became more diverse. It was not uncommon for a single crew to have several Spanish-speaking workers, as well as natives from Korea, Vietnam, Malaysia, India, Afghanistan, several countries from the Middle East, and various Eastern Europeans including Albanians, Greeks, Poles, Czechs, and Romanians.

Many workers also came from the Gold Coast, Guiana, war-torn Sierra Leone, and West Africa, as well as Somalia, Ethiopia, Uganda, and Kenya. From the Western Hemisphere, it was not uncommon to have Brazilians, who speak Portuguese, workers from any of the Latin or South American countries, and from French Canada.

In essence, the company's construction crews on many sites represented a virtual United Nations. When there were several crew members speaking the same tongue and at least one had reasonable fluency in English, foremen-to-crew relations went reasonably well. But, most often this wasn't the case. Composition of crew members varied widely from site to site, project to project, and even from season to season.

TOWER OF BABEL

After delving into the project at length, Bob realized that slightly increasing turnover rates were due at least in part to the inability of project foremen to communicate directly with individual crew members.

CAUTION

> Even kind or caring project foremen can be less effective at their jobs when language barriers diminish effective communication.

Bob thought about the history of human kind and the legions of disputes that had occurred between peoples of different nations who did not speak each other's tongue. If countries sometimes ended up going to war with one another over misunderstandings, then it made sense to believe that workers might be departing at higher rates because of their inability to express themselves adequately, to be heard and understood, to be able to appropriately express frustration or grievances, and, conversely, to receive appropriate feedback or even praise.

When Bob presented his findings to the owner, at first he was met with a rather cool reception. It couldn't be that; we have had foreign-speaking crews for years. Bob persevered and explained that ever more sophisticated project management software and construction, advancing construction methods, down time and slack time in many projects (other than the owner's task of adequately replacing the workers and getting new crew members up to speed), was at an all-time low.

Construction projects were literally being completed at a quicker pace each year, and the timing, coordination, and precision compared to past operations was a marvel to behold. In other words, operating at a more efficient pace with little or no slack also meant that there was less overall time for bonding and conversation in general. Perhaps the modern management efficiencies resulted in some type of crossing of the threshold when it came to maintaining the human touch.

After a while, the owner bought into Bob's analysis, and, then of course was most interested in the strategy that Bob had come up with to overturn the turnover. As a result of making his rounds and collecting the input of many others, and collecting articles in construction industry magazines on this very same topic, Bob developed a multipart strategy that was inspired, though rather simple and inexpensive—and the owner liked it!

Bob's plan involved having each of the foremen attend a short training program that he would design personally. The program would only take an hour and a half and only require one handout with printing on both sides of the page. The following was Bob's handout.

MOTIVATING THE SHORT-TERM CREW MEMBER

Enrique is 19 years old. He came to this country when he was 11, never graduated from high school, and has only a rudimentary grasp of English. Enrique works on one of your crews. He is a good worker, is seldom late, and hardly ever complains. You can feel it, though: He is not going to be at your establishment very long. He will pick up a few dollars and then move on—to where, you will never know.

Can you increase the job length for workers like Enrique? Indeed, can you motivate someone who, quite bluntly, toils for long hours for little reward? The answer is a resounding "Yes." It will require a little effort and ingenuity on your part; still, after all is said and done, Enrique and others in his situation may still depart on short or no notice. The odds that they will remain with the job longer, however, will increase if you follow some of the guidelines for motivating these employees.

Check Your Attitude   You need to check your attitude before any motivation program can succeed. As human beings, we broadcast messages all the time. What are you broadcasting to your crews? That they are replaceable? That you are not concerned with their needs?

It's easy for the supervisor who has watched dozens of laborers come and go to develop quickly the view that "It's the nature of the business, why fight it?" It is that attitude that partially perpetuates the massive turnover in the industry. Resolve that you can take measures to increase the average longevity of low-paid laborers and your attitude and initiative will make a difference.

An Encouraging Word   How long would it take you to learn some key phrases in Vietnamese, or the language of your low-paid laborers? Whether they speak Spanish, Korean, or Farsi, it won't take long to master some short conversational pleasantries. Many bookstores are stocked with dictionaries providing various language translations. Even easier, sit down with one of your key crew members. On a piece of paper, jot down the phonetic spelling of phrases such as "How are you?" and "You're doing a good job."

Unannounced Breaks   Periodically throughout the day, and particularly on challenging days, give your workers unannounced breaks. Augment these mini-vacations by distributing snacks. The few dollars you may spend will pay off in terms of greater productivity that day. These breaks will also enhance longevity among low-paid crew members. It pays to offer little perks.

Rotating Leadership   Rotate leadership among some crews. For instance, on four consecutive days, make sure that crew members each have one day as "foreman." For some of your workers, this may represent their first taste of leadership. Rotating leadership is most effective when the crew members are unfamiliar with each other.

Awards System   Make "contests" short in duration and high on visuals. For example, you could keep a chart on the wall or other visible location indicating who has had the most consecutive days without being absent or tardy. Which crew performances have prompted words of praise from customers? Who has gone above and beyond the call of duty in the last week?

You can easily chart and share these achievements with crew members on duty. People like to see their names on a chart followed by stars or other performance indicators. The chart could be language proof, for instance. Everyone recognizes their own name in English, and stars or dollar signs can indicate the bonuses you'll offer. After posting the charts, set up a simple system of rewards, which could include cash or more time as a team leader.

Develop Mentors   Look for leaders among your crew members who can serve as mentors to newly hired staff. This alleviates having to break in each crew member. Those individuals selected as mentors will be pleased with this special status and will not only assist in achieving smoother operations, but will help alleviate quick departures among new employees.

Use a Checklist   Here's a checklist to help you determine if you are raising or lowering morale, increasing or decreasing crew members' length of stay, and serving as a leader, not just as a manager:

- Do I make sure employees understand how to properly complete a job?

- Have I clearly indicated what results I expect?

- Do I offer adequate and ongoing support?

- Do I cultivate positive relationships?

- Do I show concern for crew members as individuals?

- Have I established appropriate recognition and reward systems?

- Do I take the time to learn and dispense encouraging phrases for enhanced communication?

Even if you practice all of the above recommendations, you still will not eliminate quick turnover or enhance crew motivation. Yet, if you can induce the seasonal crew member to stay on an extra week or encourage crew members to finish a big job on time, then you have made your job a little easier, and have contributed to the profitability and long-term viability of the company.

AFTER THE HANDOUT

Bob covered the entire sheet during this session and then requested each foreman to employ at least one of the measures with each crew member at least once a week. So, if the foremen had 15 crew members on a project, he was responsible for one of the following measures per crew per week, or in other words, an average of three such instances a day:

- Offering an encouraging word in the crew member's native tongue

- Giving workers unannounced, on-the-spot breaks

- Rotating leadership among some groups, and so on

Each project manager would then report back to Bob at the end of each week so they could assess progress. As it turned out, progress was readily visible from the first day on.

TIP

Foreign-born crew members start perking up immediately when people say a few words or phrases to them in their native language.

At the end of the first week, most foremen reported an increased level of vibrancy, higher morale, even possibly higher energy level. At the end of several weeks, the foremen were convinced that the program was sound.

At the end of several months, as they looked at the data on a project-by-project basis, the owner and Bob could see that the turnover rates were dropping. Workers were staying on longer, and they didn't need to be replaced, hence project profitability was rising. And both Bob and the owner felt great about that outcome.

The 30-Second Recap

- Researching your problem, talking to everyone who might be able to provide insight, and being observant of your environment and their environment is a strong way to be sure at the outset that your project is headed in the right direction.

- Meeting with your sources on their turf can make them more candid and open, and can help you see aspects of the project you might have overlooked entirely.

- Even the most qualified, expert professionals are only as good at managing as they are good at communicating with their teams.

- Morale and motivation among the troops can come as much from the positive attitude of management as anything else. Even a menial job can be worthwhile if there is positive reinforcement for a job well done.

LESSON 14

Learning from Your Experience

In this lesson, you learn how to keep your role as project manager in perspective, the value of mastering project management software, why it pays to keep your eyes and ears open, and how to get ready for what is next.

LIFE IS LEARNING, AND SO ARE PROJECTS

Whether you volunteered to head up your current project or were assigned to it, whether you eagerly anticipate going to work the next day or dread it, it is highly important to keep your goal as project manager in perspective. Managing a project and managing it well routinely leads to other things. These include managing larger projects, being promoted as a supervisor, manager, or department head, and earning increases in pay, bonuses, and other perks.

Maybe you were given the role of project manager because no one else was around, but more often than that, it is because someone higher up in your organization believed that you could do the job. Perhaps you are being groomed to take on even greater levels of responsibility.

TIP

Any project can be viewed as a stepping stone along your long-term career path.

No project is too inconsequential, too low a priority, or too outside of your immediate interest area to not manage effectively. Some represent large steps, some are tiny. In each case, you have several opportunities:

- Undoubtedly you will learn things along the way that you can use at other times and places in your career. What learning opportunities might develop? Learning new software, getting along with diverse groups of people, selling skills (please remember as a project manager you are always selling one thing or another at every point along the way), and a greater appreciation for your organization's processes.

- When you work with a project team you develop bonds with individuals that have potential future value as well. Perhaps they will work with you on other projects. Perhaps you will be reporting to them on projects. Their skills and interests ultimately may impact the direction that your career path takes.

TIP

If you can't stand some or all of your project staff, you can cultivate your ability to manage others effectively. Realistically, there will be lots of other times in your career where you have to work with less than "bosom buddies." You might as well hone your skills now.

- Working on a project that represents a departure from what you were doing previously exposes you to new vistas. Perhaps you get to see another aspect of your organization. Perhaps you get to deal with external elements that represent new and challenging ground for you. Perhaps you become more in tune to your own weaknesses as a manager, as a career professional, and as an individual. Many a project

manager has decided to enroll in a course or get additional
training as a result of tackling a challenging project.

- You potentially get to step into the batter's box, where all
eyes are focused on you. Taking on a project means that others are counting on you for specific performance over specific intervals. Hence, the authorizing party and stakeholders
have a vested interest in your progress.

TIP

Being the object of constant or semi-constant scru-
tiny means that you also have the opportunity to
shine in ways that otherwise might be difficult to
muster if you were simply doing routine work as
part of the rank and file.

In short, consider the opportunity to manage projects, large and small,
desirable and undesirable, as the wonderful opportunities they invariably secretly represent.

MASTER THE SOFTWARE

Project management software, discussed in Lessons 10, "Choosing
Project Management Software," and 11, "A Sampling of Popular
Programs," is applicable to far more than the project at hand. Whatever
software skills you develop on this project will be of value on future
projects, both for your organization and those you may elect to take on
individually.

Most people don't learn software unless it is critical to their performance, status, and livelihood. When everyone else was switching from
typewriters to personal computers, career professionals had no choice
but to learn some word processing software, just to keep pace with
society in general and their own industry in particular.

Today, as more people learn more Internet applications or effective ways
of accomplishing tasks, society is poised for an era of unprecedented

productivity. Yet, the majority of people who mastered traditional PC software skills such as word processing, database management, spread sheet applications, and communications don't necessarily encounter project management software. They aren't aware of its vast applications for managing all aspects of one's professional and personal life.

At home, you may discover the ability to use what you've learned on the job to do the following:

- Maintain a greater level of control of household expenditures

- Plot the path that you need to take in order to retire by a desired age

- Coordinate personal travel plans as never before

- Map out a plan that will carry your child to the finals in academics, sports, or the performing arts

KEEP YOUR EYES OPEN

How projects are initiated in your organization—by whom, when, and for what result—tells you much about the workings of your organization. Are projects routinely initiated as a result of deadlines or competitive pressures? Or, do they represent customer service initiatives undertaken by the organization to enhance its overall project or service offerings even when there is no immediate, visible pressure to do better? Forward-thinking organizations always operate according to the latter.

TIP

Forward-thinking organizations don't wait for dire circumstances to surface; they operate in a "managing the beforehand" mode, recognizing that proactive organizations stay in the lead by routinely taking leading, decisive actions.

Whether you are working for an organization that operates in a crisis mode, a leading edge mode, or someplace in between, as a result of your observations as a project manager, undoubtedly you will come across other opportunities for your organization.

The execution of your project in pursuit of the desired outcome, if you keep your eyes open, inevitably will lead to insights worth reporting back to your authorizing party and stakeholders. It also tends to lead to the formulation of new projects which, quite conveniently, probably are best managed by you. Think of it as a Machiavellian win-win situation where you are selfishly identifying what else you want to be working on, which happens to coincide with that which will benefit your organization. In this regard, you begin to take on far more control over your career path than seemed within your grasp before initiating your current project.

TIP

Effective project managers often create their own path by identifying one project after another. Such projects both help their organizations and further the project manager's own career.

Along the way, everything that worked well, added to all the road-blocks, obstacles and flat out failures, becomes grist for the mill. While you don't want to incur a series of frustrations on your current project, if you have the where-with-all to recognize that everything you experience is a lesson for another day, and can ultimately serve to benefit you in one way or another, then the current ordeal need not seem so bad.

Preparing For the Next Project

Since the effective execution of one project undoubtedly will lead to another one, what are you doing along the way to improve your capability and readiness to tackle new projects? For example, are you

- Maintaining a notebook or file on your hard drive of key project insights?

- Denoting the skills and capabilities in detail of the project staffers who contributed to the project in some way?

- Compiling a resource file of books, audio-visual material, software, Web sites, supporting organization, and any other resources that could possibly be of use on future projects?

- Establishing relationships with vendors, suppliers, consultants, and other outside product and service advisors?

- Establishing relationships with stakeholders, be they top managers, the authorizing party, clients, customers, other project managers, other project team members, department or division heads, as well as controllers, accountants, and administrative staff?

Are you pacing yourself to a practical degree so that if you are requested to jump into something else immediately after completing this project you will be more or less ready? This involves taking care of yourself, eating balanced meals, perhaps taking vitamin supplements, getting adequate rest, exercising, practicing stress reduction techniques and, in general, allowing yourself to have a life even during the course of the project? In closing, it may be appropriate to refer to the words of Rudyard Kipling in his classic poem, *If:*

IF

—by Rudyard Kipling

If you can keep your head when all about you

     Are losing theirs and blaming it on you;

If you can trust yourself when all men doubt you,

     But make allowance for their doubting too;

If you can wait and not be tired by waiting,

      Or, being lied about, don't deal in lies,

      Or, being hated, don't give way to hating,

      And yet don't look too good, nor talk too wise;

If you can dream—and not make dreams your master;

If you can think—and not make thoughts your aim;

If you can meet with triumph and disaster

      And treat those two impostors just the same;

If you can bear to hear the truth you've spoken

      Twisted by knaves to make a trap for fools,

      Or watch the things you gave your life to broken,

      And stoop and build 'em up with worn-out tools;

If you can make one heap of all your winnings

      And risk it on one turn of pitch-and-toss,

      And lose, and start again at your beginnings

      And never breathe a word about your loss;

If you can force your heart and nerve and sinew

      To serve your turn long after they are gone,

      And so hold on when there is nothing in you

      Except the Will which says to them: "Hold on!"

If you can talk with crowds and keep your virtue,

      Or walk with kings—nor lose the common touch;

If neither foes nor loving friends can hurt you;

If all men count with you, but none too much;

If you can fill the unforgiving minute

> With sixty seconds' worth of distance run—

> Yours is the Earth and everything that's in it,

> And—which is more—you'll be a Man, my son!

THE 30-SECOND RECAP

- Managing a project well often leads to managing larger projects, being promoted as a supervisor, manager, or department head, and earning increases in pay, bonuses, and other perks. Any project holds the potential to become a stepping stone along your long-term career path. Hence, avoid regarding any project as too inconsequential, too low a priority, or too outside of your immediate interest area to be managed effectively.

- Effective project managers often create their own path by identifying one project after another. Such projects both help their organizations and further the project manager's own career.

- At all times pace yourself so that if you are requested to jump into something else immediately after completing this project you will be more or less ready!

APPENDIX A
Glossary

analytical approach Overcoming challenges by chunking them down into divisible elements to better comprehend each element and ultimately resolve the issue in contrast to the systems approach.

contingency plan A backup course of action in the event that the originally proposed course of action encounters significant barriers or roadblocks.

corporate culture The sum total of prevailing practices, methods of operation, beliefs, morals, and widely held notions that tend to perpetuate themselves within an organization and which help to define, as well as limit the range of behaviors and activities available to members of the culture.

cost benefit analysis A determination of whether to proceed based on the monetary time and resources required for the proposed solution versus the desirability of the outcome(s).

critical path The longest complete path of a project.

critical task A single task along a critical path.

culture The lifestyle and prevailing beliefs of a population within a political unit, such as a community, organization, state, or nation or within an association, cyber community, or other method of affiliation.

deliverables Something of value generated by a project management team as scheduled, to be offered to an authorizing party, a reviewing committee, client constituent, or other concerned party, often taking the form of a plan, report, prescript procedure, product, or service.

dependent task A task or subtask that cannot be initiated until a predecessor task or several predecessor tasks are finished.

dummy task   A link that shows an association or relationship between two otherwise parallel tasks along a PERT/CPM network.

environment   One's surroundings; at work, one's office and surrounding offices and, in general, one's work place.

full path   The charted route on a critical path diagram for a project from the first task to the final outcome.

holistic   The organic or functional relations between the part and the whole.

micro culture   A culture within a department, division, branch or project team or within an entire corporation itself.

milestone   A significant event or juncture in the project.

Murphy's Law   The age-old axiom stating that if something can go wrong, it will go wrong.

non-critical task   A task within a CPM network for which slack time is available.

objective   A desired outcome; something worth striving for; the overarching goal of a project; the reason the project was initiated to begin with.

parallel tasks   Two or more tasks that can be undertaken at the same time. This doesn't imply that they have the same starting and ending times.

Parkinson's Law   "Work expands so as to fill the time allotted for its completion."

path   A chronological sequence of tasks, each dependent on predecessors. In terms of CPM, tasks arranged in order, with predecessor tasks preceding dependent tasks.

politics   The relationship of two or more people with one another, including the degree of power and influence that the parties have over one another.

precedence   If the completion of one event has priority over another, then that event has precedence over the other.

predecessor task   A task that must be completed before another task can commence.

project constraint   A critical project element such as money, time, or human resources, which frequently turns out to be in short supply.

project director   The individual to whom a project manager reports. Project directors maintain a big-picture focus and not a day-to-day focus on project activities on par with the project manager. Project directors may have several project managers reporting to them and hence require a series of briefings at specified intervals.

project environment   The political, legal, technical, social, economic, and cultural backdrop within which a project team operates.

project manager   An individual who has responsibilities for overseeing all aspects of the day-to-day activities in pursuit of a project, including coordinating staff, allocating resources, managing the budget, and coordinating overall efforts to achieve a specific, desired result.

project tracking   A system for identifying and documenting progress performance for effective review and dissemination to others.

risk   The degree to which a project or portions of a project are in jeopardy of not being completed on time and on budget, and, most importantly, the probability that the desired outcome will not be achieved.

scope of work   The level of activity and effort necessary to complete a project and achieve the desired outcome as measured by staff hours, staff days, resources consumed, and funds spent.

schedule   A planned sequence of events.

scheduling tools   Project management software, organizers, electronic calendars, time management software, day planners, and any other device that supports one's use of time and productivity.

slack   Margin or extra room to accommodate anticipated potential short falls in planning.

slack time   Time interval in which you have leeway as to when a particular task needs to be completed.

stakeholder   Those who have a vested interest in having a project succeed. Stakeholders may include the authorizing party, top management, other department and division heads within an organization, other project managers and project management teams, clients, constituents, and parties external to an organization.

subcontract   An agreement with an outside vendor for specific services, often to alleviate a project management team of a specific task, tasks, or an entire project.

subtask   A slice of a complete task; a divisible unit of a larger task. Usually, a series of subtasks leads to the completion of a task.

systems approach   A far-reaching cohesive way to approach problems involving varied and interdependent relationships, standing in contrast to the analytical approach.

task or event   A divisible, definable unit of work related to a project, which may or may not include subtasks.

timeline   The scheduled start and stop times for a subtask, task, phase, or entire project.

total slack time   The cumulative sum of time that various tasks can be delayed without delaying the completion of a project.

trade-offs   Options regarding the allocation of scarce resources.

work breakdown structure (WBS)   Project plans that delineate all the tasks that must be accomplished to successfully complete a project from which scheduling, delegating, and budgeting are derived. A complete depiction of all of the tasks necessary to achieve successful project completion.

work statement   Detailed description of how a particular task or subtask will be completed, including the specific actions necessary, resources required, and the specific outcome to be achieved.

Appendix B

Further Reading

Archibald, Russell. *Managing High-Technology Programs and Projects*. New York: Wiley, 1998.

Baker, Sonny and Kim Baker. *On Time-On Budget: A Step-by-Step Guide to Managing Any Project*. Paramus NJ: Prentice-Hall, 1992.

Barkley, Bruce and James Saylor. *Customer-Driven Project Management*. New York: McGraw Hill, 1994.

Cleland, David. *Project Management: Strategic Design and Implementations*. New York: McGraw Hill, 1998.

Clough, Richard and Glenn Sears. *Construction Project Management*. New York: Wiley, 1991.

Davidson, Jeff. *Breathing Space: Living & Working at a Comfortable Pace in a Sped-Up Society*. New York: Mastermedia, 2000.

———. *The Complete Idiot's Guide to Managing Stress*. New York: Alpha, 1999.

———. *The Complete Idiot's Guide to Managing Your Time*. New York: Alpha, 1999.

———. *The Complete Idiot's Guide to Reaching Your Goals*. New York: Alpha, 1998.

———. *Joy of Simple Living*. Emmaus, PA: Rodale, 1999.

Dinsmore, Paul. *The AMA Handbook of Project Management*. New York: Amacon, 1993.

Frame, J.D. *Managing Projects in Organizations.* San Francisco: Jossey-Bass, 1995.

———. *The New Project Management.* San Francisco: Jossey-Bass, 1994.

Hallows, Jolyon. *Information Systems Project Management.* New York: Amacom, 1997.

Kerzner, Harold. *Applied Project Management.* New York: Wiley, 2000.

———. *In Search of Project Management.* Wiley, 1998.

Kezsbom, Deborah, et al. *Dynamic Project Management.* New York: Wiley, 1989.

Kostner, Jaclyn, Ph.D. *Knights for the TeleRound Table.* New York: Warner, 1994.

Levasseur, Robert. *Breakthrough Business Meetings.* Holbrook, MA: Adams Media, 1994.

Lewis, James. *The Project Manager's Desk Reference.* New York: McGraw-Hill, 1999.

———. *Fundamentals of Project Management.* New York: Amacom, 1995.

Lientz, Bennett and Kathryn Rea. *Project Management for the 21st Century.* San Diego: Academic, 1998.

Mackenzie, Kyle. *Making It Happen: A Non-Technical Guide to Project Management.* New York: Wiley, 1998.

Meredith, J.R. and Samuel Mantel. *Project Management.* New York: Wiley, 1995.

Rea, Kathryn and Bennett Lientz editors. *Breakthrough Technology Project Management.* San Diego: Academic, 1998.

Thomsett, Michael. *The Little Black Book of Management.* New York: Amacom, 1990.

Verzuh, Eric. *The Fast Forward MBA in Project Management*. New York: Wiley, 1999.

Weiss, Joseph and Robert Wysocki. *5-Phase Project Management*. Boston, MA: Perseus, 1992.

Williams, Paul. *Getting a Project Done on Time: Managing People, Time, and Results*. New York: Amacom, 1996.

INDEX

A

administrative managers, 12
analyzing, arm chair, 150
anticipating problems, 18
approaching budgets, 71
arm chair analysis, 150
Artemis Prestige, 129
asking questions, 28
authorizing party, 11
avoiding micromanagement, 64
awards, 154

B

bosses, 143
    multiple, 143-145
bottom-up budgeting, 73
breaks, 154

budgets, 49, 67
    approaching, 71
    bottom-up, 73, 75
    calculating, 68
    considerations, 77-79
    crises, 70
    examples, 76
    hidden costs, 70
    planning, 75-79
    preparing, 72
    problems, 77-79
    slack, 68
    top-down, 72-75

C

CA-SuperProject, 129
calculating budgets, 68
calendars, software, 124
changing tasks, 97
charting future (Gantt charts), 88

Q-R

S

Jeff Davidson is frequently called to speak at conferences, conventions, and retreats. He has made presentations to 580 groups in North America, Europe, and Asia on topics related to staying productive and competitive, yet remaining balanced and happy while confronting constant change. Comments such as "Best of the Convention," or "Best we've ever heard," represent typical feedback to Jeff's presentations.

Jeff is the author of numerous books, thousands of articles, and nine audio and video programs. Jeff's six-cassette album, *Simplifying Your Work and Your Life* (SkillPath), which he corecorded with Dr. Tony Alessandra, gives career professionals the tools and practical information they need to address the complexity in their everyday lives.

Jeff offers a blend of keynote and seminar presentations on how to maintain balance while remaining profitable and competitive. His presentations include

- Relaxing at High Speed™

- Managing Multiple Priorities

- Overworked or Overwhelmed?™

- Handling Information and Communication Overload

In recent years, several of Jeff's speeches (including "Relaxing at High Speed," "Choosing when it's Confusing," "Overworked or Overwhelmed?" "World Population and Your Life," and "Handling Information Overload") have been published in issues of the prestigious *Vital Speeches of the Day,* alongside those of Dr. Henry Kissinger, Lee Iacocca, William Bennett, Michael Eisner, and Alan Greenspan.

The Washington Post, where he's been featured eight times, called Jeff Davidson a "dynamo of business book writing." Millions of people have read about Jeff in *USA Today,* the *Los Angeles Times,* the *San Francisco Chronicle,* and the *Chicago Tribune,* or have seen him featured on *Good Morning America, CBS Nightwatch,* CNBC, *Ask Washington,* and hundreds of regionally based talk shows.

To obtain a comprehensive list of resources, including additional information on Jeff's keynote and breakout presentations and Jeff's speech availability, visit the Breathing Space Institute's Web site at www.BreathingSpace.com, fax to 919-932-9982, e-mail jeff@BreathingSpace.com, or call Jeff directly at 919-932-1996.